We Were Really There

We Were Really There

The Rebirth of Manchester City

DAVID BERNSTEIN
with Tim Rich

pitch

First published by Pitch Publishing, 2024

Pitch Publishing
9 Donnington Park,
85 Birdham Road,
Chichester,
West Sussex,
PO20 7AJ
www.pitchpublishing.co.uk
info@pitchpublishing.co.uk

A CIP catalogue record is available for this book
from the British Library.

ISBN 978 1 80150 690 8

Typesetting and origination by Pitch Publishing

Printed and bound in Great Britain by TJ Books Ltd, Padstow

Contents

Introduction 9

89.25 13

Bar Mitzvah Boy 25

Decline and Fall 37

In the Hot Seat 56

If You Don't Make Dust, You Eat Dust 71

Money 100

The Bubbles Burst 110

Anatomy of a Tackle 127

A Parting of the Ways 137

The Keegan Effect 155

The Lifeboat 182

'Chairman, Are You Sitting Down?' 196

An Untenable Transfer 214

Epilogue: Into the Arms of a Dictator 232

Afterword 252

Bibliography 254

To the wonderful supporters of Manchester City who made the journey from third-division football to world champions

Introduction

I HAVE been extremely fortunate to have had a career in business spanning 60 years which is still continuing. It has included many highs but nothing to equal the intensity, pleasure and satisfaction of my nine years at Manchester City and particularly the last five as chairman. I had supported the club since I was 11 and had never imagined that 44 years later I would have the opportunity to help regenerate this great sporting institution.

After considerable reflection, I decided that I owed it to myself and to anyone with an interest in the history of Manchester City to record my account of that period. For me, it revisits a period in my life that was unique, rewarding and life-enhancing. For fans of City and football generally, it recalls a moment in time when a much-loved major club, which had fallen on hard times and was languishing in the shadow of its illustrious neighbour, was reborn.

It is also a case study of engendering change. From many years of working with highly talented, creative people I observed that success comes to those who love their product and are committed to the highest levels of quality and service. The financial benefit to them is secondary, a consequence of achieving excellence. At City, our team was driven by a passion for the club and a desire to build something of which we could be really proud and where the word club really meant something. Manchester City was not then a global institution but a club shaped by those who worked there. It was big enough to make a significant difference to many lives but small enough to put your arms around.

The relevance of Manchester City's rebirth between 1998 and 2003 has been hugely magnified by the incredible success achieved by the club over the last ten years. City has become the most powerful club in England, if not Europe. Although my colleagues and I planned for success, none of us could have dreamt of winning multiple trophies or achieving last season's Treble nor that our neighbours, Manchester United, would be left trailing in our wake.

Our success was, of course, a team effort. I was most fortunate to be surrounded by a small, talented and committed group. My sincere thanks, therefore, to Alistair

Mackintosh, Chris Bird and Dennis Tueart, who were all valued board colleagues. To John Wardle and David Makin, whose backing was crucial when resources were dangerously stretched. To Bernard Halford, who was second to none in his loyalty to our club. To Joe Royle for achieving back-to-back promotions and setting in motion the all-important momentum which was to carry us so far. And also, to Franny Lee for his vision and undoubted commitment to our club. Finally, to Shaun Goater and Dave Wallace for their contributions to this book. There were, of course, many others and I have tried to reference them within the book wherever possible.

This book is focused on my time at Manchester City, but my involvement in football has continued. After I left the club in 2003, I was asked to join the board of Wembley Stadium just before construction of the new ground began. I chaired the development committee and then the board of Wembley itself. The stadium was opened in 2007 and remains one of the world's iconic venues. I was appointed chair of the Football Association in 2011 and had an extremely eventful 30 months before having to retire because of an age limit. One of my proudest achievements was – at the request of the prime minister, David Cameron – to lead a review into diversity and discrimination in football. We produced a report with 100 recommendations which were signed off by every major football organisation and which has largely been implemented.

In the following years, I became increasingly concerned about many aspects of our national game and particularly the power of the Premier League and the consequential imbalance between that league and the rest of football. This problem has been compounded by a weakened FA, a predominance of vested interests and lack of independence in the governance of the English game. I worked with a distinguished group to produce the *Manifesto for Change*, the central recommendation being the need to appoint an independent regulator for English football. This has been taken up by the government in the form of a White Paper and should be incorporated into law in 2024.

My involvement in football has lasted around 30 years but nothing compares with the unique experience of being chairman of Manchester City.

David Bernstein,

Finchley, November 2023.

89.25

WEMBLEY FORMS a huge part of my life. Although I was born in Lancashire and fervently supported Manchester City, I grew up in London, a few miles from the Empire Stadium, as it was then called. I would in time become chairman of a very different Wembley Stadium and then chairman of the Football Association. On the day of my bar mitzvah, the Jewish coming-of-age ceremony, I had watched black-and-white television pictures of Manchester City winning the 1956 FA Cup. Thirteen years later, I was there in person to see Neil Young's goal win the cup again.

I was there for Dennis Tueart's overhead kick that overcame Newcastle in the 1976 League Cup Final. My last journey to Wembley as a City fan had been the night in 1981 that had seen Tottenham's Ricky Villa dance his way through a blue-shirted defence in an FA Cup Final replay to score one of the great goals seen in the stadium. It was a magical memory, except if you supported City.

However, on Monday, 30 May 1999, I was sitting in the Royal Box as chairman of Manchester City, who were wearing not sky-blue shirts but yellowy-green with black stripes. As a fixture, it seemed on a much lower level than the FA Cup and League Cup finals. This was a Football League Division Two play-off final between Manchester City and Gillingham. The winner would be promoted to what – in the days when I had gone to Wembley to see the teams of Malcolm Allison, Tony Book and John Bond – would have been called the Second Division. A few days before, Manchester United had lifted the European Cup and completed the Treble. This, surely, was one of football's sideshows.

Except that for importance, this match, watched by 76,000, eclipsed any previous game Manchester City had ever played. In the space of three years, the club had collapsed out of the Premier League and been relegated again to land in the third tier of English football for the first time in its history. It was a measure of how far the club had fallen that, until that season, we had never before played Gillingham. I had been chairman for 14 months. Unlike my predecessor,

Francis Lee, I had not played for City or brought titles back to Maine Road. There would be no latent goodwill or nostalgia to protect me should things continue to fall apart.

Before the final, Francis had given an interview to the *Daily Express*. He was at a country club in Hampshire. He had just played 18 holes of golf and was talking to the journalist with a glass of champagne in one hand and a cigar in the other. He thought there should be no pressure on Manchester City. 'I don't go in for all this stuff about pressure,' he said between puffs. 'There is no pressure on somebody playing a match if he can play the game [well]. It's wonderful. You should just go out there and enjoy it, especially at somewhere like Wembley.'

However, despite Francis's words, there was plenty of pressure. In those 14, sometimes desperate, months since succeeding him, I had begun a programme of reform to modernise the club, shore up its finances and make it a credible sporting institution. There had been long negotiations to move to a new stadium that would host the Commonwealth Games in three years' time. That stadium, the City of Manchester, now the Etihad, would become the lifeline that would eventually see Manchester City win the Treble in 2023. That future, a future we could not imagine, would have been imperilled by defeat in this 'sideshow'.

In the first leg of the play-off semi-final, at Wigan, we had fallen behind to a ridiculous, self-inflicted goal in the opening minute. I was sitting in the directors' box next to our manager, Joe Royle, who reflected afterwards that I had turned 'instantly grey' when we conceded after 20 seconds. He added: 'Bernstein knew better than anybody how utterly crucial it was for City to escape the wilderness at the first attempt, for failure to do so would torpedo the board's plans to rebuild the club's fortunes.'

Had we lost, Manchester City would have survived. There would, though, have been deeper cuts into the fabric of the club. Our credibility as tenants for Manchester's newest stadium would have been severely damaged. The enormous support from the fans – which had sustained us in our fixtures at Wycombe, York and Stockport – would inevitably begin to bleed away. All season they had chanted 'We're not really here' in self-mocking disbelief that one of English football's great institutions had been reduced to this. But we were here now. And we had to win.

When I became chairman in March 1998, the *Manchester Evening News* commented that I had 'come out of the shadows' to rescue the club. Had we lost, we would have remained deep in those shadows. For how long, nobody knows, but it would have been long enough to have swallowed many of our ambitions.

Royle, who four years earlier had come to Wembley with Everton and beaten Manchester United to win the FA Cup, had treated the match as one of the most important of his career. Because our training ground at Platt Lane was so open, training had been shifted to Maine Road to preserve secrecy. Bill Beswick, a sports psychologist who would go on to work with England, had been brought in to speak to the players. Since December, led by Andy Morrison, a fisherman's son who had grown up in Devon, and Shaun Goater, a striker from Bermuda who had once been on Manchester United's books, we had lost only twice and I was confident we would not lose now. In the semi-finals, Gillingham had overcome a Preston side managed by a young David Moyes. Preston may have been a bigger threat. We had comfortably beaten Gillingham a few weeks before at their Priestfield ground.

Before taking my seat in the Royal Box, I ran into Gillingham's chairman, Paul Scally, who remarkably told me that, whatever the result, his manager, Tony Pulis, would be leaving the club on the final whistle. There had been fierce disagreements over what Pulis saw as non-payment of his bonuses from player sales. I messaged Joe to let him know there was some disharmony in the opposition camp he might be able to exploit.

At the start of the game, pride and optimism battled with the inevitable nerves, but we never really got going. Out there, on Wembley's vast pitch, City lacked fluency and composure. We struck the post a couple of times but, as the last ten minutes approached, it was a scrappy, tense, agonising affair. At 0-0 there was nothing remotely enjoyable about it. There was too much at stake.

And then, in the 81st and 87th minutes, Gillingham scored. My heart sank. I was looking at the giant Wembley scoreboard – Gillingham 2 Man City 0 – and all I could hear was the Gillingham fans singing 'Going up, going up, going up!' The royal blue flags of Gillingham were waving. The light blue ones were scattered around the feet of our supporters. This was not going to finish well. All around me and in our end, our fans started streaming out. A mass exodus. Looking back later on the TV recording, I recognised a lot of the faces and it wasn't disappointment I was seeing, it was complete distress.

There was no time for happy endings. I sat there like a statue, a blank look determinedly fixed to my face. I was always conscious of not betraying my emotions but inside I was shaken, asking myself: 'What the hell are we going to do next season? Another year in the third tier is going to be more than difficult.' We had worked so hard to get our credibility back and we would have to start all over again. The second attempt to get out of the division would be much more difficult. On the bench, Royle, who had watched Scunthorpe win the League Division Three play-off the day before, turned to his assistant, Willie Donachie, and said: 'It's Scunny next season.' Resignation, frustration and despondency were swirling around.

As I looked down, Ian Bishop had the ball deep in our half on the right. Frantically trying to get something going, he saw Richard Edghill on the other flank. Bishop was coming to the twilight stage of his career but he was still the best passer in the division. Yet even he, summing up our day and the desperate urgency of the situation, lost his usual poise and sprayed it too far ahead of his team-mate. It was sailing into touch for a Gillingham throw-in which would have given them another opportunity to eat up time. Suddenly, needlessly, and ultimately miraculously,

Mark Saunders in the Gillingham midfield lengthened his stride. Had he reached the ball, I suppose, he could possibly have run through on our goal or taken it to the corner flag. Instead, it was inches beyond his instep and, though he got there, the ball brushed his studs and went out for a throw-in for us. When that ball went over the touchline, it was the 25th second of the 90th minute of the game. The digital clock on the scoreboard read 89.25.

From the throw, we worked it infield back to Bishop. This time he played it forward, 25 yards along the ground. Paul Dickov, as impishly clever as ever, stepped over it and drew his marker with him. Our other substitute, Gareth Taylor, accepted the pass and laced it on to Goater. He was 20 yards from goal. The Gillingham keeper, Vince Bartram, who had just been named man of the match over the Tannoy, raced out and he and a defender converged to block Goater's low shot. They had done exactly the right thing but the collision wiped both of them out. So, when the ball rebounded to Kevin Horlock to the left of the D, Bartram was stranded. Horlock, with supreme self-possession at such a frenetic moment, calmly drilled a left-foot shot into the net. 'Ah well,' I thought. 'Another brick in the wall of "typical City". Too little, too late.'

Before Gillingham kicked off, the fourth official raised the board showing five minutes of stoppage time. All sorts of conflicting thoughts hit me. 'Maybe? No. Surely not …' With 90 seconds left, City's Dutch centre-half, Gerard Wiekens, clipped a 60-yard diagonal ball upfield. Taylor went up to win the header, nodding it down to Horlock, who fed the Goat. Shaun had scored 21 goals that season and naturally took on the shot from 20 yards but there was no gap as a Gillingham defender hurled himself into the line of fire to thwart him. The ball struck his legs and spun off to the right … to Dickov.

Paul had become one of my favourite players but he was not what you would call a world-class finisher. However, Joe, who had been a fine striker for Everton, Manchester City and England, had been working one-on-one with Paul, coaching him to settle himself and pass the ball into the net. And when the moment came, Dickov passed it hard – but passed it nonetheless – side-footing it into the roof of the goal.

Given the magnitude of the circumstances, his calmness when the ball fell his way was astonishing. At that point, my mask slipped. A poker face was beyond me. Sheer elation hit me, followed by a wave of relief. We had looked into the abyss, with all its implications for finances, the new ground, hanging on to our best players, the spirit of goodwill we had restored, City's profile and general credibility. And by the skin of our teeth, we had clawed it back. Dickov's goal was wondrous in every respect, the highlight of my sporting life.

In extra time, we played a lot better and could have won it. One extraordinary thing was the sight of our end filling up again as fans swarmed back into the stadium. Fortunately, the Wembley staff, showing great common sense, did not try to prevent a mass re-entry of those who had left in despair with City on the brink of defeat. I heard of one fan who left at 2-0 and drove all the way back to Manchester, refusing to turn the radio on and confront his disappointment. He did not learn how it had all unfolded without him until he walked into his home that evening.

At 2-2, of course, Gillingham could easily have snatched it but, at 2-0 up with hardly any time remaining, Pulis had withdrawn his strikers. Watching those 30 minutes of extra time was not pleasant but when the referee blew the final whistle I was very confident that we would win the penalty shootout. Having seen the miracle that saved us unfold, we simply could not lose this match now.

Only one moment threatened my certainty. At 1-0 up in the shoot-out after Nicky Weaver had saved Paul Smith's first penalty for Gillingham, diving to his right but improvising late to block the shot down the middle with his feet, Dickov took his turn. When they were at Arsenal together, our striker and Bartram, the Gillingham goalkeeper, had struck up such a firm friendship that they had been each other's best man. Dickov had beaten him once but this time his penalty hit the inside of the post, rolled along the goal line, struck the foot of the other post and stayed out. The emotional swings were almost unbearable. That torment did not last long. Adrian Pennock blazed wide, Terry Cooke stepped up for us and scored and, after John Hodge and Richard Edghill had both converted, we led 3-1.

Gillingham's Guy Butters had to score to keep them in it. It was a firm shot but, betraying his nerves, was hit at waist-height barely a yard to thc right of centre. Weaver dived, saved and set off to hurdle the hoardings, waving his arms to beckon his team-mates to follow and led them on half a circuit of the old greyhound track until our captain, Andy Morrison, wrestled him to the turf for a pile-on. There was bedlam around me, too. The excitement, the hysteria, the release of tension was simply incredible.

Eventually, the players came up the steps to the Royal Box and I embraced every one of them. It was never my style to get into the thick of it with the players but that time I wanted to go on to the pitch to thank the fans. On the Wembley turf, in the midst of this euphoria, Morrison came over and said: 'Chairman, you won't forget about my bonus arrangements, will you?'

Bar Mitzvah Boy

IF THE play-off final was the most important game in their history, my first view of Manchester City was another Wembley occasion which has become part of the club's collective memory.

5 May 1956 was blisteringly hot. Manchester City would be playing Birmingham City in the FA Cup Final. It was the day of my bar mitzvah when, just before my 13th birthday, I would come of age. I would read from the Torah – the first five books of the Bible. The Torah would then be carried around the synagogue for the congregation, which included my parents and extensive wider family, to respect and perhaps kiss.

My parents were only mildly religious but the occasion and the reception afterwards would be a hugely important day for our family. I was more interested in slipping away to watch the final on television. As it was the Sabbath, watching anything on television was frowned upon, especially on your bar mitzvah. The rabbi was well aware of my passion for Manchester City; he had wished me luck for the game in his sermon.

I was allowed to watch one of Manchester City's great afternoons. It is remembered not for the goals from Joe Hayes, Jack Dyson and Bobby Johnstone, nor for Don Revie's masterful midfield play, but for City's goalkeeper Bert Trautmann playing the last 17 minutes of the match with a broken neck. His courage was such that the victory speeches delivered from the balcony of Manchester Town Hall were drowned out by a crowd chanting for a man who had inspired huge demonstrations against him outside Maine Road when he signed for the club in 1949, five years after fighting for Germany in the Wehrmacht. The demonstrations had only been called off after the intervention of Manchester's chief rabbi, Alexander Altmann. Now, Trautmann's heroics only cemented my love for the club.

Manchester City should not have been my club. I was to live most of my life in north London. Tottenham and Arsenal were the obvious teams to support. At my school, Christ's College, Finchley, I was City's only fan. The more my schoolmates mockingly pointed this out, the more entrenched my love of the club became.

I was born in Lancashire although St Helens, where I spent the first two years of my life, is closer to Merseyside than Manchester. However, there was something about City – the sky blue of their shirts, the sheer size of Maine Road, which had accommodated 84,569 for an FA Cup tie against Stoke in 1934 – that drew me in. It would never let me go.

My father was an immigrant, born in Hungary in transit from Odessa, which before the First World War was one of the most significant Jewish cities in the Russian Empire. However, Odessa was also the centre of regular anti-Jewish violence and, two years before the outbreak of war, with his wife already pregnant, my grandfather decided to leave for Britain. On their way west, my father, Henry, was born in Budapest in 1912.

He was one of nine children. His brother, Joe, would fight in the North African desert and in Italy during the Second World War. Not long after D-Day, Joe crossed the Channel and ended the war at the liberated Bergen – Belsen concentration camp, where because of his ability to speak Yiddish he stayed on as an interpreter.

Henry Bernstein grew up to run fashion shops. He met my mother, Anne, and they lived a peripatetic existence, never staying too long in one place. They went first to

Lancashire, where I was born on 22 May 1943. After the war, they moved to Bexhill, perhaps thinking the Sussex coast and sea air would be a good place to bring up a young boy. However, my parents were metropolitan people and Bexhill had no Jewish community to speak of. They moved to stay with my aunt in Wembley, then with my grandmother in the East End and eventually settled in Mill Hill in north London. However, I greatly valued my northern roots. I suppose distance breeds enchantment. I certainly had a romantic view of those 'dark, satanic mills'.

Whereas my father was one of nine and my mother one of eight, I was an only child, happy in my own company. Christ's College was a grammar school in Finchley. I was in the same year as Charles Saatchi, whose family had recently left Iraq, where they had correctly anticipated a wave of anti-Jewish persecution. Charles was a character, entranced by American pop music, who left with two O-levels. He would go on to revolutionise the London advertising scene. Above us in the school was Bobby Wilson, a great tennis player and a real hero of mine who would reach four Wimbledon quarter-finals between 1958 and 1963. Tennis was to become a passion. When he was 12, my son, Peter, lost narrowly to Tim Henman in the final of a national schools' championship at Wimbledon. I enjoyed cricket, opening the bowling for the school. I was an enthusiastic, rather than a talented, footballer.

I married my wonderful wife, Gill, in 1966. She has been a fantastic support and whatever contribution I have made to Manchester City would not have been possible without Gill. Her father, Harry, had a menswear store on Tottenham High Road and among his customers were many Spurs players including the great Double-winning side of 1961. Gill's long-term, staunch support for Tottenham Hotspur was compromised while she focused on our battle to rejuvenate City. Similarly, my four sons, Lawrence, Peter, Richard and Nick, were hugely supportive and greatly enjoyed being so close to the action. When I became chairman of Manchester City, the phrase 'typical City' was a byword for the kind of ill luck that regularly undermined the club. In 1961, I went to Luton to watch one of the first instances of 'typical City'. Denis Law managed to score seven times and still finished on the losing side.

Manchester City were leading 6-2 – all scored by Denis, who played like a god on a pitch that resembled a ploughed field. Then with 20 minutes left, the rain became a deluge and forced the match to be abandoned. The tie was rearranged for the Wednesday night and Luton won, 3-1.

Law, who scored Manchester City's only goal, remarked that the pitch at Kenilworth Road was in an even worse state than it had been when the first match was called off.

I would watch Manchester City when they came to London but it was not until March 1966 that I saw them in the flesh at Maine Road; an FA Cup quarter-final with Everton that finished in a goalless draw. On a dark, sombre day, I was drawn by the power of the crowd which, to me, resembled the pictures I had seen from the 1930s. Amid the vastness of Maine Road, I felt an immediate link with the club's past. Law was by now at Old Trafford and Manchester City were in the Second Division but Colin Bell, who had just turned 20, was already one of the most beautifully stylish footballers the club would see. It would take two replays before Everton won through. They would overcome Sheffield Wednesday in the final.

Two years later, Manchester City had gone from the Second Division to champions of England. Coached by Malcolm Allison, they were the most exciting team in the country. With Mike Summerbee running a fashion boutique alongside George Best, they were pretty stylish off the pitch, too. They were real lads with a togetherness that endured over the years. The following season, I would be at Villa

Park to see Tommy Booth's goal overcome Everton in the FA Cup semi-final and at Wembley to watch Neil Young win the cup against Leicester. They wore the red-and-black stripes, inspired by Allison's love of AC Milan. It occurs to me now that for three of Manchester City's most memorable Wembley triumphs – in 1956, 1969 and in the play-off final in 1999 – they did not wear sky blue. I watched the 1956 final on a black-and-white television but they wore claret shirts with thin blue stripes.

There was no encouragement to join the family business which, in any case, was too small to accommodate me. However, I had always felt comfortable with numbers and, after leaving school, I became a chartered accountant, studying for four years at Robson, Rhodes in the City of London. I then joined a firm called Bright, Grahame, Murray and Co. By the age of 26 I was a partner. By the time I was 35, I was a senior partner, dealing with a lot of public company work, as well as mergers and acquisitions, at a firm which was big enough to be interesting but small enough to be personal.

One of my clients was Stephen Rubin. His family had come to Britain from eastern Europe and settled in the North West, founding the Liverpool Shoe Company. When his father died, Stephen took the firm over and renamed it Pentland Group. In 1981, Pentland paid $77,500 for a 55 per cent stake in Reebok, which had been founded in Bolton, manufacturing running shoes, and which now had American owners. Ten years later, after Reebok had revolutionised sporting fashion, particularly for women, Rubin sold his stake for $770 million. There is a story of a headmaster who invested £1,000 in Pentland shares. Within ten years, they were worth a million.

Pentland was based in Finchley and Stephen Rubin asked me if I would leave the practice and join him as the company's joint chief executive. As an entrepreneur, Stephen was opportunistic and backed his gut instincts. When I went to the United States to visit Reebok's headquarters, which were now in Boston rather than Bolton, I was amazed by the scale and efficiency of an operation that, for a time, would overtake Nike as the world's biggest sportswear firm.

Manchester City were travelling in the other direction to Pentland. They had beaten Newcastle to win the League Cup in 1976 and finished second to Liverpool in the First Division the following season. But then came a decline, culminating in relegation in 1983. In the years to come, they would yo-yo between the top two divisions. I had never seen myself as anything more than a fan but now I wrote to the chairman, Peter Swales, asking if I could be of assistance. He agreed to meet me at Highbury before City played Arsenal. Swales was polite but dismissive. City lost 4-0.

When working with Stephen Rubin my role was primarily strategic development and troubleshooting. Pentland had this hugely valuable stake in Reebok and a scattering of other interests. We had to decide whether we were a sports and leisure group or a conglomerate with a range of varied interests. One of those interests involved a personal guarantee from a businessman in the north and Stephen asked me to sort it out. I always tried to deal very civilly with people rather than issuing threats and demands. I was chatting with this man when he told me he knew Mike Summerbee and, through Mike, he was aware that Francis Lee was looking for investment to launch a takeover of Manchester City. Would I be interested in talking to him? How could I not have been?

I met Francis at the Mere Country Club in Cheshire, owned by Stephen Boler, who was Manchester City's most significant shareholder. Francis explained his plans and I told him that I would write to him. He could take or leave the advice. I wrote him a long letter advising Francis that his proposals were under-capitalised. In other words, he did not have enough money to do what he said he would do.

Francis did not take my advice. At our first meeting at the Mere, he came across as someone supremely confident in his own abilities. Early on in our relationship, I played a round of golf with him at the Mere. It was a classic game and we came to the par-five 18th level. I hit three fantastic shots to reach the green but, inevitably, Francis, under pressure, struck two perfect shots to record a birdie and win the hole and the match. As one of football's great penalty-takers I should not have been surprised at his match-winning coolness.

Francis was a man who had succeeded in almost everything he had done. It was his goal on the final afternoon of the season at Newcastle that proved decisive in Manchester City winning the championship in 1968. It was his penalty that helped win the Cup Winners' Cup in 1970, which until Pep Guardiola's men won the Champions League in Istanbul was City's only European trophy. When Swales sold him to Derby against his wishes, Francis responded by winning the championship in his first season at the Baseball Ground. He had played for England and, after football, he had become a successful businessman and racehorse owner. Why would he not be confident? Why would Manchester City fans not want their club to be run by someone like this? I thought he, rather than myself, would end up as chairman of the FA. He was football's golden boy.

His campaign to wrest control of Maine Road from Swales was called *Forward with Franny*. Ousting Swales, who had been chairman for 20 years, proved a messy business. Fans supporting Francis besieged the stadium. It became impossible to stage board meetings at Maine Road. After five months, Francis took control in February 1994. Blue balloons were released over Maine Road to signal what he and many others believed would be the beginning of a brave new world, one in which Francis predicted champagne would be the staple beverage. At his first annual general meeting at a suite at Manchester Airport, Francis told the assembled audience that they should get used to trips to the airport as Manchester City would be playing regular European football.

It was a brave new world, but not, however, a successful one. There was no upswing in results. Instalments for the transfers of Keith Curle and Terry Phelan from Wimbledon

– who cost £6m between them – still had to be paid. That summer, Maine Road's most famous stand, the Kippax, was due to be demolished to meet the requirements of the Taylor Report, which demanded all-seater stadia in the wake of the Hillsborough disaster. Rebuilding the Kippax would not be complete until October 1995, would cost £16m and would reduce Maine Road's capacity by 8,000. Perhaps Francis did realise he was under-capitalised and perhaps that is why he invited me to join the board.

Decline and Fall

MANCHESTER CITY was owned by an eclectic group of shareholders, although whether they were the right people to be running Manchester City was another matter. In February 1994 I would invest £300,000, which would give me a few per cent of the shareholding, though it was not enough to be meaningful.

The biggest shareholder had been Stephen Boler, whose company, Limelight, included Dolphin Showers and Moben Kitchens. His great interest was wildlife conservation; he owned the Tswalu Kalahari Reserve in South Africa, which was to take up an increasing amount of his time. At board meetings, he was represented by a proxy, Ashley Lewis. Francis was now a substantial shareholder, although over time that percentage would be diluted. The pub chain Greenall's owned nearly 14 per cent of the club. In 1995, the club would be publicly floated on the Stock Market, creating thousands of small shareholders, the vast majority of whom would be Manchester City fans.

Among the other significant figures was Ian Niven, who during the Second World War had been a Chindit commando – parachuted behind Japanese lines. He was so partisan he could never bring himself to mention the name 'Manchester United' out loud. He always referred to them as 'Trafford Rangers'. He sat behind me in the directors' box and many would be the occasions when, with a minute to go before the final whistle with City two or three goals ahead, I would turn to him with a highly nervous enquiry: 'Surely, we are okay? Tell me we can't lose now, Ian.'

Freddie Pye was a Rolls-Royce-driving scrap metal merchant who had been manager of Altrincham, chairman of Stockport County and Wigan Athletic and vice-chairman of Manchester City under Swales.

On the periphery was Sidney Rose, a surgeon at Withington and Wythenshawe hospitals in Manchester and a talented pianist. Sidney had been a squadron leader in the RAF during the war and had cared for the Manchester United players who had survived the Munich disaster. Once, when crossing the Atlantic in the *Queen Elizabeth*, he was called on to perform emergency surgery on a passenger with a burst appendix. He asked for the liner to be stopped and, afterwards, was congratulated by one of the passengers, Winston Churchill. In the 1969 FA Cup semi-final against Everton, Mike Doyle, City's centre-half, suffered a dead leg just before half-time and Sidney made the decision as to whether he could continue.

Another memorable personality who became an honorary president was Tudor Thomas. He and his lovely wife, Mary, had supported City since they came to Stockport from Wales in 1950. He generously helped the club with important projects and, both at Maine Road and the Etihad, had an area (appropriately named the Tudor Room) where he entertained many, including match officials and scouts, surrounded by the Manchester City memorabilia he had collected. His son, Stephen, said of him: 'City was his life, his number one, even above his family.'

One outstanding servant of the club was the secretary, Bernard Halford. He had a wide range of duties, including all matters of football regulation, especially player transfers. He had joined the club in 1972 and his experience was invaluable. I used to join Bernard on wet and windy midweek evenings to watch our reserve team playing at Hyde United in matches far removed from the glamour of the first team, attended by a smattering of hopeful agents and scouts plus a handful of often elderly, always passionate, supporters who enjoyed the hot tea available.

In May 1994, the club's total annual turnover was £8m, around three times smaller than Manchester United's. Its staff costs, the majority of which would be player wages, came to £5.5m. The wages-to-turnover rate was 68 per cent, which was edging towards unacceptably high levels. None of those players' contracts contained a relegation clause. In his first annual report as chairman, Francis wrote: 'The cost of us staying in the Premier League, together with inherited transfer-fee commitments, have produced the club's worst-ever trading results. The majority of the trading loss (£6.08m) relates to the deficit on transfer fees for the year of £5,689,025. The underlying trading performance of the club is unsatisfactory given the club's level of support and action has been taken, in particular with new executive appointments to maximise the club's commercial potential.'

For the first time, the club had a chief executive, Colin Barlow, who had played as a winger for City before going into business. His main task was to prepare the club for flotation on the Stock Market, something Manchester United had successfully done in 1991. In the boardroom, Francis could be a dominating presence. The people he gathered around him were, frankly, not up to running a major football club in a fast-changing world. That Colin Barlow had played for Manchester City did not make him the best-qualified person to be the club's chief executive.

As chairman, Francis had some visionary qualities. He wanted Maine Road redeveloped with three new stands similar to the new Kippax, each with restaurants and corporate boxes. He was quick to see the value of foreign footballers, bringing in Uwe Rösler and Georgi Kinkladze. He recognised early on just how lucrative the Premier League would be.

Francis did not, however, recognise the importance of a new training ground. Manchester City had trained at Platt Lane since 1979. Then, it had been the headquarters of the Manchester Police Athletic Club while City trained at either Maine Road or Cheadle Town. The club bought Platt Lane in conjunction with Manchester City Council, who could and did use it for their own events. The facilities were not up to scratch. Richard Edghill, who first trained there as a teenager, remembers Platt Lane for the alcoholics who hung around outside. Frank Clark remembers it for the canteen which was not run by the club and which used to serve chips with everything.

For a vision to be successful, you have to have stability and, as Manchester City lurched from one crisis to another, we became so caught up by the present that it was impossible to prepare for the future. You cannot plan an extension when your house is on fire and for any of Francis's plans to come to fruition, it was imperative that Manchester City remained in the Premier League. Once we were relegated, matters spiralled out of control.

When I joined the board, Brian Horton was the manager charged with keeping the club on course. Horton kept City in the Premier League in his two seasons in charge but there was no serious challenge for trophies. Horton had been appointed by Swales and even then he knew it was a precarious position – Swales had advised Horton not to buy a house in Manchester because his job would not be secure enough to justify it. He knew Francis would want his own man. In May 1995, he was dismissed, although the first Horton knew about it was from the back page of the *Daily Mirror*.

As he came down to breakfast at the Sopwell House hotel after the League Managers' Association annual dinner, he was shown the paper by Frank Clark, who two years later would also be sacked. Clark would discover his fate via a sports bulletin he was listening to on his car radio.

For his first managerial appointment, Francis drew up an interesting list of possibilities, though I was not enthused by the inclusion of Alan Ball. My influence then was, however, not great. Among the candidates that Francis considered were Ron Atkinson, Alan Hansen, the former Liverpool captain who had become an exceptional football pundit, and Brian Kidd, who had played for both Manchester clubs and was then Alex Ferguson's No.2 at United.

The timing was not right for Atkinson, who had just joined Coventry, while Hansen told Francis he was only interested in managing Liverpool. Ball had just left Southampton and Francis was closer to him than to any of the other candidates. They were both Bolton boys and had played together for England in the 1970 World Cup in Mexico. He was the one appointed. I did not feel his record inspired confidence. Alan had kept Southampton in the Premier League but there had been relegations at Portsmouth and Stoke.

The season began with one point from the opening six fixtures. It was this start that was to doom Manchester City.

There was a recovery but the final match of the season, at home to Liverpool, arrived with City needing to better either Southampton's result against Wimbledon or Coventry's against Leeds to survive. It was a match that defined this era at Manchester City, with Steve Lomas wasting time by the corner flag, believing a 2-2 draw was enough to keep City up while Niall Quinn, who had been substituted, ran along the touchline yelling at him that we still needed another goal. In the days before smartphones, Francis had been told via a woman in the directors' box listening on a transistor radio that Southampton were losing. He had passed that completely wrong information to Ball in the dugout. The chain reaction that followed was typical City.

When any organisation enters turbulent waters and serious changes are needed, it is vital that not only is relevant action taken but that those changes are communicated effectively and confidently. Relegation certainly required this approach. It could have been a catalyst for fundamental change.

We did not address relegation either fundamentally or cosmetically. Champagne was still served in the boardroom. Francis was determined to keep Ball as manager but, after defeats at Bolton and Stoke left City 19th in League Division

One – as Division Two had been renamed – Francis asked Ball to call at his home near Manchester Airport and dismissed him over cigars and glasses of Scotch whisky.

You could measure Francis's power by the way in which managers were appointed. The decision to hire Ball had been entirely his. Perhaps the fact he had just become chairman and the sense that he had the overwhelming backing of the club's fanbase meant it was natural the first managerial appointment should be his. However, the choice of Ball's successor was much more collegiate and, later, when it came to appointing Joe Royle in 1998, Francis had little input.

George Graham was seriously considered but chose to join Leeds. Dave Bassett had the personality to deal with a club like Manchester City and had narrowly failed to promote Crystal Palace to the Premier League, losing to Leicester in the play-off final. However, in 1987 he had quit as Wimbledon manager because the chairman, Sam Hammam, interfered in team selection and he suspected Francis would do the same.

When I met Steve Coppell at my home in Finchley, I thought we had the man who might begin the revival of Manchester City. He interviewed very well. He seemed confident and competent. He was young, having just turned

41. He had taken Crystal Palace to the FA Cup Final in 1990 and to third in the league the following year. He knew the region, having grown up in Liverpool and played for Tranmere and Manchester United. He was intelligent and articulate. I thought I had found the man to manage Manchester City for many years to come. He lasted 33 days.

After a few games, Coppell simply disappeared from view. Francis told me: 'He's gone back to London and I can't get hold of him. Can you talk to him?' Coppell agreed to meet me in a hotel in the capital, where he seemed in a highly distressed, nervous state. He sat in his room while telling me he simply could not cope with the situation he found himself in. I said: 'Steve, if you want some time off, we can arrange that and get your number two [Phil Neal] to take charge for a while.' We were very keen to keep him but Coppell looked like a man under enormous strain. I never discovered what had triggered it. Perhaps he found the scale and problems facing Manchester City to be utterly overwhelming.

He told me that he wanted to quit the club and we had no alternative but to call a press conference announcing his departure. The assembled journalists were shocked by how ill Coppell looked and no questions were allowed. At a board meeting, Ashley Lewis asked if future managers should be given a medical before their appointment. Francis said he would consider it. Three months later, Coppell returned to Crystal Palace and promoted the club to the Premier League. I found the whole affair mystifying.

The club was being run by caretaker managers. Asa Hartford had taken over from Ball and seen City knocked out of the League Cup by Lincoln. Neal took over on 8 November. City were then 16th, six points off a play-off place and 12 from automatic promotion. By the time Clark came up to Manchester as Coppell's permanent replacement, we were 21st and one point from a relegation place.

By now I was vice-chairman. I was becoming more and more involved in the running of the club. Francis and I were now speaking every day and I would see him at his home, Stanneylands, whenever I was in Manchester. I sometimes stayed at Stanneylands, where Francis and his wife, Gill, would be very hospitable. To both of us, Frank Clark seemed a good appointment, maybe the best we could get at the time. Frank was used to pressure.

He had replaced Brian Clough at Nottingham Forest and promoted them back to the Premier League in his first season. In his second, he had steered them to a third-placed finish.

I picked up Frank from Piccadilly Station on 29 December and drove him to Platt Lane to meet the players. Because I knew that Neal had still not left the training ground – he was saying his goodbyes to the squad – I parked as far away from the reception as I possibly could and told Frank we should wait. Eventually, I had to confess that the reason why we were waiting was that his predecessor had not yet left the building. It was not the ideal way to start.

Frank did try to change things. Hearing that the players had not had a Christmas party for ten years, he organised a belated one in January and brought his guitar, dedicating a song to Francis, who had come along. It was called 'Worried Man Blues'. Clark complained the team bus had no facilities for serving hot food to players on away trips. All we could offer were sandwiches. That could be changed. The fact that Manchester City had a squad of 50 players, half of whom would not even get a reserve game, was more difficult to rectify.

By now, we were desperate for money. There had been very little financial reserves to fall back on when we were relegated from the Premier League. In February 1997, there was a rights issue – where existing shareholders are allowed to buy more shares – to raise £11m. Stephen Boler took advantage of it to become once more Manchester City's largest shareholder. Francis's shareholding fell to 11 per cent. More significantly, John Wardle and David Makin became the club's second-largest shareholders.

John had founded JD Sports in 1981 with David, who was then just 16, selling discounted sports clothing from a shop in Bury. Two years later, they moved into Manchester's Arndale Centre. The year Wardle bought into Manchester City was the year that JD Sports was floated on the Stock Exchange. By the time they sold the company to Pentland in May 2005, JD Sports had 329 outlets. John was a publicity-shy man but I think he liked the glamour of being involved. David, who had watched City from the Kippax, was a much more outspoken character but disliked formality and had no interest in joining the board. As Manchester City continued to flounder, he became extremely agitated and eager to stir the pot. There were times when I had to take him aside and say: 'Look David, Francis is doing his best and I have confidence in him. You need to back off.' In fact, my confidence in Francis was beginning to fray but these were opinions I kept to myself.

Clark's initial results had been good. City did not lose any of their first nine games under his management and we ended the season 14th. It was, nevertheless, the lowest finish in Manchester City's history and it was a record that would not stand for long.

A substantial part of the funds raised from the rights issue was invested in players. The club's transfer record was broken to sign a striker. We paid Portsmouth £3.25m for Lee Bradbury, who could not cope with the pressure of playing at Maine Road where the crowd turned on the players very quickly as the disappointments piled up. We did not win at home until 27 September. The game began with only goal difference keeping City out of the relegation zone. We beat Swindon 6-0. Our only other win had come at Nottingham Forest, who would go up as champions.

Wardle and Makin had brought Dennis Tueart on to the board. Although they had both played for Manchester City, Lee and Tueart's time at Maine Road overlapped by only a few months and they were not close. Tueart had enjoyed a good relationship with Swales and unlike some former City players – most notably Mike Summerbee – he had not supported the *Forward with Franny* campaign.

Tueart met Makin and Wardle at Maine Road on 22 November 1997 following a 1-0 win over Bradford. Makin complained that Francis dominated board meetings and he felt there should be someone else around the table who had specialist football knowledge.

The following month, Dennis gave an interview to the *Mail on Sunday*, who pointed out that Manchester City were, in terms of league position, the fifth club in Greater Manchester behind United, Bolton, Stockport and Bury. Tueart told the paper's football correspondent, Joe Melling: 'I will make my recommendations as quickly as is feasibly possible. If those recommendations are not accepted, then I will be wasting my time. Anyone who knows me will tell you I am not the kind of guy who accepts his time being wasted.'

Melling wrote: 'Despite the disgraceful degeneration of one of the most hallowed clubs in the English game, the fans continue to demonstrate an almost unbelievable stoicism in refusing to desert them. Average gates at Maine Road are around 30,000 and the huge army of support clogs the motorways to back the team away from home. But their perilous position close to the bottom of Division One has also brought demonstrations of an uglier kind.'

This included the fans chanting: 'I'd rather be in Barnsley than Barbados,' mocking Francis's frequent trips to the Caribbean. Francis was in Barbados when that interview was published four days before Christmas. Despite the winter sunshine, all the confidence and charisma appeared to have drained away from him upon his return. The pressure from the fans, from results and from the bank seemed intolerable, even for such a naturally courageous man. I chaired one or two meetings at this time, mainly those concerned with funding, which was becoming a serious issue.

At a board meeting before Christmas, we had to come to terms with reality. Manchester City were 16th in the table and would almost certainly not be promoted back to the Premier League. This meant we would lose £1.7m of Sky TV money and our kit supplier, Kappa, would reduce its sponsorship payments. I told the board it was 'an absolute necessity' for the wage bill to be reduced as the club was now close to its overdraft limit. Clark had agreed to raise £500,000 in player sales – this was in the days before the transfer window. We failed to sell a single footballer. In two months – September and October – the club accounts showed a loss of £357,000. Since the start of the season our losses stood at £5.8m.

Everything came to a head on Valentine's Day 1998. Manchester City lost at home to Bury. Fans came on to the pitch and one of them tore up his season ticket in front of the bench and the directors' box. We were in the relegation zone and this was more than David Makin could stand. He had been at the Mottram Hall hotel in Cheshire, listening to the game on the local radio station, GMR, and asked to be put through to their football phone-in. With 3,000 fans demonstrating outside Maine Road, Makin told GMR listeners that Francis was a dictator and that Clark's tactics as a manager left much to be desired. He finished the interview by demanding Francis's resignation.

Three days later, the board voted to sack Clark. Francis played very little part in our decision to ask Joe Royle to succeed him. Tueart knew Royle would be interested because, not long before, Joe had phoned him and, according to Dennis, told him he had a chance of two jobs. One was managing Northern Ireland, the other was at West Bromwich Albion. Before he committed to either, he wanted to know the managerial situation at Manchester City.

Now there was a vacancy, Tueart phoned Royle and arranged a meeting with Joe, himself and John Wardle at a friend's house in Rochdale. Joe, who had been successful as manager at both Oldham and Everton, was informed that not only had Clark not yet been told of his dismissal, but Francis had also wanted to keep faith with him. He was then told that Francis would not be chairman of Manchester City for much longer.

I had been approached by Wardle and Makin and asked if I was prepared to become chairman. I knew Francis's credibility was shot to bits and I told them that, provided I had the support of the shareholders – particularly Boler and Greenall's – I would be prepared to take over. Over a long business career, I have had to deal with many sensitive and difficult situations but this was really tough. I had worked closely with Francis for nearly five years and had a high regard for him. He had done his utmost to cope with an extremely difficult situation.

On Saturday morning, 14 March, I went to his house with Ashley Lewis, as the representative of Stephen Boler, Manchester City's leading shareholder. I told Francis directly: 'I'm sorry but this is not working.' I emphasised he no longer had the confidence of the shareholders and the board and should resign. Four months before, Francis had told the press that he would stay on as chairman until Manchester City were back in the Premier League and that he would jump off the top of the Kippax if the club was relegated again.

Now, however, I think there was a part of Francis that was relieved that it had come to this. He seemed ready to go.

His hand-written resignation letter was faxed over the next day. In it, Francis recalled how, before every game he played at Maine Road, he would stand in the tunnel, puff out his chest and tell himself he was the best player on the pitch. He wondered why the present generation of Manchester City footballers did not have that same self-belief. I left his house feeling unusually stressed. I drove to Port Vale to watch City lose 2-1 in pouring rain.

In the Hot Seat

CRISIS IS an overused word in football but there was little doubt I had become chairman in the midst of perhaps the deepest crisis in Manchester City's history. We were 22nd in the old Second Division, with eight games to go, one point and one place from safety. The position immediately above the relegation line was occupied by Tranmere, who had played two games fewer. Nevertheless, I did not think we would be relegated. We were still Manchester City, with all its history, resources and fanbase and, Tranmere apart, there were five other clubs, who, although above us, led by fewer than five points – Portsmouth, Port Vale, Huddersfield, Bury and Queens Park Rangers. I thought we would do it. Even before the final game of the season, at Stoke, I believed we would survive.

This, however, was the inheritance I was handed. At the final board meeting Francis chaired, the last one before

I became chairman and the first Royle attended as manager, the situation had been grimly sketched out. The players' wage bill for January 1998 was £161,000 over budget. The Co-operative Bank had increased the overdraft facility to £6.75m. They required £1m-worth of player sales before the transfer deadline at the end of March, otherwise Francis and I would have to give financial guarantees of £800,000 and £200,000 respectively. Boler indicated he was considering disposing of his 21 per cent stake in the club. We had also received a letter from a firm of structural engineers, Marston and Grundy, stating they were not prepared to guarantee that the roof of the North Stand was safe. Repairs were not completed until March 1999.

Amid all this, there were two rays of light. Chris Bird, a PR consultant who had worked with JD Sports since 1989, gave a presentation to the club about how its chaotic public relations might be improved and Royle asked permission to approach Sheffield United to sign Willie Donachie as assistant manager. Both were hired and Chris and Willie, in their different ways, would help transform Manchester City.

On the Monday after the defeat at Port Vale, the club had called a press conference to announce my appointment as chairman. Before it began, I went into the chairman's room. I told Chris Bird that I was not used to large press conferences and would prefer to do the interviews on a one-to-one basis. Chris, a tough professional from east Manchester, said: 'Are you kidding? There are a hundred journalists out there.' I agreed to speak from the top table and then took questions. Halfway through, I thought to myself: 'I can do this.'

The *Manchester Evening News* described me as 'a man stepping out of the shadows'. The paper remarked that there would now be 'less hype and more focus on reality rather than former glories'. When asked how I was feeling, I replied: 'I am very excited by the challenge ahead but a little nervous as well. It is not exactly the easiest job in football.'

Given the fact that Manchester City had gone through four managers in four and a half years, Janet Royle had been firmly against her husband taking the job. Since the previous two chairmen had been driven out amid a background of fan unrest, my family had questions to ask me as well. The position of chairman was an exposed one – literally so, since at Maine Road you sat in the front row of the directors' box and next to season ticket holders. Gill had her doubts but was very supportive once I had made my mind up to do it.

Our four boys, who ranged in age between 20 and 27, were thrilled.

What would I do now I was in the chairman's seat? I had been a director for more than four years but I had been no back-seat driver. I had largely been involved with shoring up the finances of the club. I did not fill my head with thoughts of what I might do should I ever become chairman of Manchester City. I recognised the people whom Francis had assembled around him were not good enough. As chief executive, Colin Barlow had been replaced by Mike Turner, who had been Liverpool's commercial manager, but his performance had not impressed me.

I realised John Wardle and David Makin were powerful people who had been instrumental in Francis's resignation. John was respectful and always called me 'chairman', never 'David'. He was very supportive.

Shortly before I agreed to become chairman, Makin had met me in London. I was then chairman of French Connection and we saw each other in our flagship store in Regent Street. He was sounding me out to see if I would be suitable to take over from Francis. He was very flattering towards me, though I knew from his reputation just how volatile he could be. His reaction to the defeat by

Bury meant those outside the club, particularly the media, knew as well.

Football is a vindictive business but, as the board assembled at Maine Road for its first meeting without Francis, I emphasised that he should be treated with dignity and respect. Francis had been a great player for Manchester City. As chairman, he had led from the front and exposed himself to stress and abuse which had taken their toll. My remarks were particularly aimed at Dennis Tueart. He and Francis were alpha males. They had both played for Manchester City and England and they had both been successful businessmen. The fact was, once Francis recovered from his ousting as chairman, he did try to interfere, particularly over team affairs. The day after his resignation was announced, he phoned the *Manchester Evening News* to warn me publicly not to make radical changes to the club's academy. There was never any question that I would. In April, after a 1-0 defeat at home to Birmingham, he wrote to me asking that Georgi Kinkladze should be included in the side.

'He [Kinkladze] informed me he was 100 per cent fit and 100 per cent committed to helping the club out of its current position and I therefore implore you to ask your director of football to please ask the manager to bring him into the squad or I fear the director of football could be directing us into the Third Division. I hope sanity prevails!'

We did not have a director of football, although Francis considered this was a role Tueart occupied in practice – he had been appointed to the board because of his specialist football knowledge. When he was chairman, Francis would sometimes telephone his manager, Brian Horton, the evening before a game and query his team selection. This was something I had no intention of repeating. Royle did not want a director of football and, in time, would come to object to Dennis's presence at the training ground.

Kinkladze had come to Manchester from Dinamo Tbilisi in 1995. The fans adored him and sang songs in honour of a footballer whose passing and vision sometimes appeared on another plane to his team-mates. Francis had an almost paternal attitude towards him while Alan Ball thought Kinkladze could transform Manchester City in the way Matt Le Tissier had transformed Southampton. However, Kinkladze scored a fraction of Le Tissier's goals and was a liability defensively. Frank Clark believed

Kinkladze was a luxury in the kind of squad Manchester City possessed in 1997/98 but concluded that neither the fans nor the board would tolerate his being sold.

Joe made up his mind quickly and decisively. In his opening game, at home to Ipswich, he stationed Kinkladze on the right. Kinkladze moved to the left, created City's opening goal, ignored his manager's instructions to go back to the right wing and left open the space that Ipswich exploited to win 2-1. Joe concluded there could be no place for Kinkladze in his team. He was recalled for the final game of the season at Maine Road, where he scored against Queens Park Rangers with a free kick, but effectively his Manchester City career was done.

He would be sold to Ajax for £4.75m in the summer. At a club where they had extolled the virtues of technically gifted footballers since Johan Cruyff made his debut, Kinkladze made little impact.

In February 1999, Francis wrote to me again, this time suggesting the board needed 'an experienced football-minded person to pass on much-needed expertise which is currently lacking on the current board'. By this, Francis presumably meant himself and he stated there were many other 'large shareholders' who shared his opinion.

out of his depth. He used to get lost driving around Manchester because he didn't know the city, which rather summed up his time with us.

Chris Bird: My first experience of Manchester City was being knocked off the white wall that went around the Kippax. I would have been five and it would have been in the 1968/69 season when City were the reigning champions. I was watching a reserve-team game in which Tony Book was coming back from injury. He cleared a ball which hit me and knocked me clean off the wall. After the game a policeman came over and told me that Tony Book wanted to see me so, accompanied by my brother and his mate, we crossed the pitch and went up the tunnel and we walked into a room that had a rope across it where Colin Bell, Franny Lee and Tony Book were playing head tennis. Tony just wanted to apologise for hitting me. That was my introduction to Manchester City. The next time I walked up the tunnel, I was a director of the club.

I got into PR and worked for JD Sports. I got them a sponsorship deal at City and in 1997 I was doing a football event called 'Legends at Lunchtime' where you would have footballers talking about the game after a business lunch at Maine Road. I wanted to book Alan Hansen. I didn't know Dennis Tueart but I did know he had a lot of contacts in the game and would have a number for Hansen. He came to the lunch and, afterwards, asked me what I thought of the club.

I told Dennis it was a shambles: 'It leaks like a sieve. Every time I pick up the paper, there's someone different being quoted from Manchester City. Everyone's speaking to the press. You need tightening up.'

I told him I would give him six months of my time for free. Dennis told me he would get me to do a presentation to Francis Lee and the rest of the board. When I walked into the boardroom, it was like a Jacobean banquet. There was food and drink everywhere.

After I'd made my presentation, Francis said: 'I don't think that's going to work. If a journalist rang you at three in the morning with a story about one of the players, what would you do?'

I said: 'I'd ask the journalist to hold on to the story until I could check it out and deal with the player and then I'd ring the journalist back.'

Francis said: 'They wouldn't do that; they would just run the story.'

Nothing much happened and a couple of months later, I got a call from Dennis saying that they were going to sack Frank Clark and appoint Joe Royle. Could I deal with the media? Shortly after that, there was another call from Dennis, saying Franny was going, David Bernstein was coming in and could I arrange the press conference?

I was having a cup of tea with David before the press conference and he offered me the job of Manchester City's media liaison officer. I told David I couldn't do it because I ran my own PR company, to which he replied: 'Could you give us six months?'

After I'd done six months, David said: 'Could you have a look around the club and tell me what you think?' I was given a role in how Maine Road was run, the catering, all sorts of things. I changed a lot. When they got rid of the chief executive, Mike

Turner, David asked me to step up to become chief operating officer.

One of the first events I had to organise was the AGM at the Bridgewater Hall. Usually, at these things, people would stand up and shout questions at Bernard Halford, Peter Swales or Franny Lee. We needed to be more professional and so I was miked up, took the questions and ran the AGM as you would expect a professional company to run its business.

If You Don't Make Dust, You Eat Dust

MANCHESTER CITY'S relegation to what most people thought of as the Third Division was an utter humiliation but, in many ways, it was a blessing in disguise. There was now a real element of fear around Maine Road, among the fans and in the boardroom. There was no appetite for internal dissent. Manchester City may have dropped two divisions in as many seasons but they could go lower. Between 1984 and 1986 Wolverhampton Wanderers, a club with a similar history and fan base to Manchester City, had been relegated from the First to the Fourth Division in successive seasons. That element of fear helped give me a free hand – or a much freer hand than I might otherwise have enjoyed. There could be no more papering over the cracks.

I quickly organised an interview with the *Manchester Evening News*, in which, under the headline 'A Blueprint for Revival', I detailed how we were going to change fundamentally as an organisation. A number of supporters told me that it had given them a glimmer of hope in the darkest of times. We also implemented changes that were cosmetic but which demonstrated that the old order could not carry on. We had to show we were serious and there could be no sacred cows. Just because someone had played for or had a friend on the board at Manchester City, it should not guarantee them a job at the club. Recruitment had to be based on ability.

One of the anomalies of Manchester City was that the club did not have a boardroom. It had been turned into a room where female guests were entertained before matches. Because of the demonstrations against the board that plagued the chairmanships of Peter Swales and Francis Lee, board meetings were sometimes moved from Maine Road. If they were held at the ground, we would meet in the restaurant. I was determined that the board of Manchester City should meet in an authentic boardroom. The boardroom table was a magnificent piece of furniture that had been stored in a cellar. We had it brought up, polished and displayed in all its glory.

There was a serious intent behind this. There is a mystique about a football club's boardroom which could work to our advantage when holding meetings or conducting negotiations. Even our bank manager was slightly daunted when entering the Maine Road boardroom.

I wanted people sitting around that table because they had clearly defined roles, not just because they had a passion for Manchester City. Chris Bird joined the board to advise us on PR and provided considerable energy. Bryan Bodek was appointed because he was a lawyer and, given the scale of the changes I wanted to make, we would need legal advice. Alistair Mackintosh came on to the board at the age of 28. He was a chartered accountant and would help oversee the financial restructuring of the club.

In October, Stephen Boler suffered a fatal heart attack as he boarded a plane at Johannesburg that would have taken him to his game reserve. He was just 55. Although he was Manchester City's largest shareholder, Boler's interests had been increasingly focused on wildlife conservation. His death removed a strong character from the club who might have become an alternate focus of power to Makin and Wardle.

One of the sadder aspects of Francis's chairmanship had been the alienation of Colin Bell from the club. The man who could claim to be Manchester City's greatest player had worked with the club's youth academy. Frank Clark had not thought Colin was up to the job and replaced him with Jim Cassell, who had been Oldham's chief scout and would run the academy until being sidelined shortly before the Abu Dhabi takeover. However, Clark recommended that Colin be given an ambassadorial role. Francis, however, wanted Colin out of the club completely. Bell was removed, creating a rift that was so deep it was never to heal. Colin died in 2021 without ever speaking to Francis again.

I decided that Colin should be brought back into the club and, in July, we announced he would be returning as an ambassador, representing the club in the hospitality suites at Maine Road and dealing with clients. Colin had wanted a more football-related role, either as a scout or as a consultant, but the idea was rejected. We kept on Mike Summerbee, whose personality was very suited to entertaining corporate guests, but our circumstances meant I had to write to him to tell him his fees were being reduced. I resolved not to be paid by City and travelled economy class. In contrast to our relegation in 1996, champagne would not be served in the boardroom until Manchester City were back in the Premier League.

We had to try to reduce a squad bloated by the signings made by three former managers. None of them had a relegation clause in their contract. Georgi Kinkladze's sale to Ajax may have raised £4.75m but some transfer deals had to be more creative. We would offer buying clubs deals where we would pay a third of the player's wages for a year or we would spread the instalments out over a number of years.

The club offices were still based in what was once a house in Hart Road in Moss Side, where it looked like nothing much had changed since Manchester City won the FA Cup in 1934. The cost of moving the offices into the stadium was £101,000. The builders, Fernley Construction, agreed to do it in return for £24,000-worth of hospitality. Provided some of the office space was given over for a schools' studies project, we would be eligible for grants worth £30,000 over three years. Effectively, we would make a profit of £6,000 on the move. In the situation Manchester City were in, we had to think on our feet.

Two divisions above us, the Premier League was monetising football as never before. In December 1994, Manchester United opened its Megastore that would end up attracting 10,000 customers for its merchandise every matchday at Old Trafford. City, meanwhile, ran a souvenir shop from a space the size of an average living room. David Makin had complained about the inadequacy of the shop facilities as early as October 1996 but nothing had been done.

The only suitable space I could see for a club store at Maine Road was to the left of the main entrance. It was a social club run by Greenall's and I persuaded them to clear it out and let us have it. They would be paid with 100,000 shares in the club. In the shape of John Wardle and David Makin, we had men who were experts in fitting out sports shops and they enthusiastically threw their weight behind the project. The City Superstore did not quite compare with the Megastore for sales but it was a huge upgrade on what had gone before.

Very early on, Joe Royle came to me and said: 'Chairman, this training ground we've got is completely unacceptable for a serious football club.' After overseeing several training sessions at Platt Lane with fans looking through the wire-mesh fences, Joe thought it resembled performing inside a zoo. He added: 'I won't be at Manchester City forever but one thing I can leave behind is a proper training ground.'

We explored buying up sites in Timperley near Altrincham and another in Didsbury before turning our attention to Carrington, a greenfield site to the south of Manchester. United were already committed to moving their training ground to Carrington after Sir Alex Ferguson argued their ground at the Cliff in Salford was too small and too open to the public. City's Carrington development was built quickly and built well. Joe was still at the club when it opened in 2001.

Because Carrington was on greenbelt land, we had to undertake surveys on the impact on wildlife and the trees on the site. There was also a public right of way running alongside the ground. For the sake of privacy and because the lack of privacy had been a key issue at Platt Lane, we tried to block off the path. However, our legal advice was that the footpath was regularly used and that, in the words of our lawyers: 'The footpath societies, such as the Ramblers' Association and the Peak and Northern Footpath Society, always ardently oppose any plans which result in the total loss of a public right of way.' They advised us not to proceed.

The public right of way would prove especially troublesome for Roberto Mancini when he became

Manchester City manager as it allowed photographers to use stepladders to see over the hedges we had planted and take pictures of his training sessions. When these degenerated into fights with his leading striker, Mario Balotelli, the photographers had pictures that would interest those putting together the front as well as the back page.

The training ground pitches had the same turf as that used at Maine Road. It had a gym and would eventually have a hydrotherapy pool. It opened 18 months after work began. Platt Lane still boasted excellent pitches, on which Manchester City's academy teams trained and played until November 2014. By then, Carrington was already becoming surplus to requirements as the club prepared to move all its training facilities to the superlative surrounds of the Etihad Campus.

It amazed me that the club had taken so long to address the shortcomings of its training ground. Liverpool had begun training at Melwood in 1950, although it was not until Bill Shankly's arrival in 1959 that the ground was transformed. In 1951, Manchester United had taken over the Cliff, which had floodlights before Old Trafford did. Until 1979, Manchester City trained at Maine Road, Cheadle Town or at Wythenshawe Park, which was a public open space in south Manchester. The attraction of Platt Lane was that, by sharing the facilities with Manchester City Council, the club would be eligible for Sports Council funding. It was a cheap solution to a serious problem that the men who had run Manchester City for nearly a quarter of a century never properly addressed.

Contrary to Francis's warning that we would run down the academy, we actively invested in Manchester City's future. The academy was the one area that was not subject to cutbacks. In Jim Cassell, we had someone we knew could mould young players. Under Cassell's guidance, Shaun Wright-Phillips, Micah Richards, Stephen Ireland, Daniel Sturridge and Joey Barton would emerge.

I made the decision to promote Chris Bird and Alistair Mackintosh to the posts of executive directors; I had asked Mike Turner to leave his position as chief executive in November 1998. Chris and Alistair both showed themselves early on to be extremely bright and extremely able. They were from differing backgrounds and they complemented each other well. Chris was extrovert and more flamboyant; Alistair was lower profile but a great example of an iron fist in a velvet glove. Chris was dynamic, energetic and could be tough with the media while forging good relationships with them. Chris persuaded the board to allow *The Times* access to all areas of the club for a weekly feature on how Manchester City were coping with life in the third tier of English football. He argued it was the only way the club would command regular coverage in the national media.

Chris had just joined the club when I became chairman but Alistair was someone I recruited. We knew we needed a financial director. We advertised for one, drew up a shortlist of five, interviewed them all and didn't like any of them. We had a second round of recruitment and I interviewed Alistair at my home. He already had a job lined up with *The Economist*. I offered him the post in 45 minutes and he immediately accepted.

Alistair proved to be an exceptional appointment. He was hard-nosed and a good negotiator. He went through the club accounts and revised them into a simple format that everyone in the boardroom and beyond could understand. He helped inspire confidence in the club because people who dealt with Alistair realised they were dealing with a serious person and serious people had been in short supply at Manchester City. When we began negotiations to move to the new stadium, he was heavily involved. He was a reassuring presence to have by your side when dealing with Sport England and the city council.

We decided early on to be as open with the fans as we could. Our AGMs were held at the Bridgewater Hall, Manchester's foremost venue for classical music. At many clubs, supporters who came to AGMs to ask questions were seen as irritants. I resolved to give the supporters who owned shares – 471 of whom turned up – as much time as they needed. At the Bridgewater Hall, one of the directors turned to me and said: 'They've had 30 minutes asking questions. I think that's enough.' I said: 'No, the fans have come from all over the country, perhaps just to ask one question. We should allow them to do it.'

Manchester City had been a club that leaked information constantly. The media would be given conflicting and often contradictory accounts from multiple sources inside Maine Road of where the club was headed. We created an environment where at board level there were strict protocols as to who could give statements to the media. It meant the club spoke with a unified voice and that directors were accountable for their comments. This was symptomatic of the professional and cohesive way in which we were beginning to operate.

In August 1998, the board met just as Manchester City were embarking on their adventure in the third tier of English football. It says something for how the club was regarded that the safety officer reported he had been unable to secure sponsorship for the stewards' jackets, which used to be sponsored by Chubb. We had asked the bank for an overdraft of £5m, which we anticipated would rise to £6m as the season reached its climax. The Co-op Bank had replied that our request 'should be realistic so long as the team performed successfully and gates were maintained'.

We had already been given an indication of what was to come. A crowd of 32,134, a record for the division, had come to Maine Road to watch Manchester City beat Blackpool 3-0. Sales of the matchday programme netted £20,000, which was a figure the club had last reached when it was in the Premier League. It set a pattern that would last the season, particularly away from home. Nineteen of Division Two's clubs had their biggest gates of the season when City came calling. After a direct-mail campaign, targeting 10,000 businesses across the North West, corporate bookings were running at 95 per cent of the previous season's. Nearly all the boxes in the Kippax had been sold two months before the season began. Merchandising sales were running ahead of budget. Despite being in the third tier, Manchester City's website was in the top ten most-visited in English football. The fans, whether in suits or in City shirts, were doing their bit.

However, as Joe and I travelled the motorways to supporters' clubs around the country in October and November; a time of defeats at Lincoln and Wycombe, it was becoming clear that, while the support may have been exceptional, the results were not.

The nadir came in December. On the 8th, Manchester City appeared for the first and only time in the Auto Windscreens Shield, losing 2-1 at home to Mansfield in front of a crowd of 3,007, the lowest ever to watch a first-team game at Maine Road. On the same night, a few miles away, Manchester United were facing Bayern Munich in the Champions League at a sold-out Old Trafford.

The *Daily Mirror* used photographs of the grounds to illustrate how wide the gulf now was between the two Manchester clubs. The next time a reporter from the *Mirror* came to Maine Road, Chris Bird had to usher him away for his own protection as some supporters threatened the journalist with violence. Eleven days later, we lost 2-1 at York. We were 12th in League Division Two, with seven wins from 22 matches. The gap between City and the two automatic promotion places was 15 points. With half the season remaining, we were looking at the play-offs as our likeliest – and probably only – way out of the division.

It was around this time that Joe asked me to speak to the players. When he was chairman, Francis Lee would sometimes go down to the dressing room after matches and give a speech to the team. This was something I would never have dreamt of doing. I took the same approach in business – don't try to do the job of the person you are employing to do it.

However, our increasing concerns resulted in Joe asking me to address the players. Not long before, I had been in America doing some business in Indianapolis on behalf of Pentland, for whom I was still working – I took no renmuneration for my work with Manchester City. There, I was presented with a framed poster of a rodeo rider, his horse kicking up plumes of dust in the arena. The slogan said: 'If You Don't Make Dust, You Eat Dust'. It's a sentiment that, in my business life, I have tended to agree with and I took the picture with me to Platt Lane and showed it to the players when I spoke to them. I added: 'We have been eating dust for too long – let someone else do the eating.'

I don't know what impact, if any, this made on them but Shaun Goater did remind me of it when I celebrated my 80th birthday 24 years later.

On Boxing Day, we went to Wrexham, where Richard Edghill recalls Manchester City playing some of the worst football of any side he has been involved with. As the team travelled to Wales, another player, Michael Brown, believed his manager would be sacked if City lost. This was not true. I was completely convinced Joe was the right choice. Whenever a director asked if it was time for a change I would reply: 'There has been enough change at this football club.' I was naturally nervous at the way things were progressing, but behind the scenes we seemed to be doing everything right. Importantly, however badly we played at the Racecourse Ground, we won 1-0.

Many believe the next match, at home to Stoke, was one of the catalysts for the club's transformation. It was on a Monday night and we went into the interval a goal down to a crescendo of boos. The patience of the fans, who had been remarkably supportive, seemed to have dramatically snapped. There was also an explosion of anger in the dressing room that threatened to spill out of control. Whatever words were said, they had an effect.

Paul Dickov equalised two minutes after the restart and the winner arrived five minutes from the final whistle. In the five months that followed, we lost just twice – at home to Oldham and Wycombe, who ended the season having done the double over Manchester City. In those 24 games after Boxing Day, City won 15, drew seven, scored 44 times and conceded 12.

A couple of months into the season, I received a call from Crystal Palace saying their chairman, Mark Goldberg, would like to speak to me. When he was put through, Mark told me that Palace were very interested in Lee Bradbury and we arranged to meet on neutral territory in London to discuss the transfer.

Goldberg drew up outside the hotel in his Rolls-Royce. When he asked me about Bradbury, who had cost Manchester City £295,000 for every league goal he had scored, I did the usual talk-up of the player: 'We think very highly of him, he is a great lad who has been very unlucky but, of course, we are always open to a deal.' The figure I had in mind was £600,000. I said to Mark: 'I think we are going to need £800,000.'

'David,' said Mark, banging the table. 'I will give you a million.' It was an irrational action, motivated by vanity or ego, and presumably the desire to impress the Palace fans. It is not often someone offers you 25 per cent more than you asked for but Goldberg, who had only just taken over at Selhurst Park, wanted a headline figure. Crystal Palace had been relegated from the Premier League and Goldberg decided on a vastly expansionist policy, appointing Terry Venables as manager alongside Steve Coppell as director of football and selling ten per cent of the club to Juventus.

The headlines were big but the results were small and, in January, the club collapsed into administration with £22m of debts. Bradbury was sold to Portsmouth, where he had begun his career, for £300,000. By then, Crystal Palace's administration meant that we had difficulty getting the final instalments of that transfer. In August 1999 we were still awaiting a payment of £280,000.

If November 1998 saw the departure of Bradbury, a man who, however unfairly, became associated with Manchester City's decline, it witnessed the arrival of someone who would be the symbol of the club's revival. Andy Morrison was not obviously destined to become a hero at Maine Road. He was a 28-year-old centre-half and City were his fifth club. He had deeply suspect knees and his binge-drinking had turned into alcoholism.

Three months after arriving at Manchester City, Morrison, who found great support from Willie Donachie, would start attending AA meetings. He has not touched alcohol since.

Morrison was, however, a born leader who galvanised the dressing room and provided the steel City required on the pitch to deal with a division that had so many rough edges. It was not a coincidence that no sooner had Andy bedded into the team that City began the upswing that would take them back to the Premier League.

We paid Huddersfield £80,000 for him. To put that into context, the following month we received a £75,000 facility fee from Sky for broadcasting a forgettable FA Cup tie with Darlington. It was an indication of how highly we rated him that when, in March, he had to attend an FA hearing in Sheffield after picking up 11 yellow cards, he was accompanied by Joe Royle, Dennis Tueart and the club secretary, Bernard Halford. Usually, a club would send only a single representative.

We rounded off the fixture list with a 4-0 win over York to finish third behind Walsall and Fulham, managed by Kevin Keegan and funded by Mohamed Al Fayed. We would have to endure the play-offs.

Our first game would be at Wigan, who under the ambitious chairmanship of Dave Whelan were preparing to move into a new stadium. This would be their last match at Springfield Park, a ground of corrugated iron roofs that had hosted Wigan County, Wigan United and now Wigan Athletic all in the shadow of rugby league. In the television commentary of the game, they were described as being financially more stable than Manchester City. Some 9,000 of our fans had gathered at Maine Road to watch the first leg on a big screen.

They would have been confident and so was I. We had finished third, Wigan had finished sixth, 11 points behind us. We had beaten them home and away and, as I sat down in the directors' box beside Joe, who was holding a bag of sweets, I had no clue of what was to follow. Twenty seconds after the start, there was a routine throw-in that both Gerard Wiekens and Nicky Weaver left for each other and, in the confusion, Wigan striker Stuart Barlow scored. Joe turned to me with his sweets and said, very calmly: 'Peppermint, Mr Chairman?'

For the first but not the last time in the play-offs, Paul Dickov came to City's rescue with an equaliser. In the second leg at a tumultuous Maine Road, Shaun Goater sealed the tie with a goal that Joe thought might have come off his arm or his chest. When the referee asked Shaun if he had handled the ball, he very properly replied that he had not. The goal stood and Manchester City moved on to Wembley for perhaps the most extraordinary game in their history.

While we had planned and trained intensively for the play-off final, once we had beaten Gillingham, there was nothing arranged. The players had to travel back to Manchester and, because I lived in London, I ended up in a Chinese restaurant in Hendon with eight others including Alistair Mackintosh. For such a momentous game, it was something of an anticlimax.

Joe and I decided we would not have a parade to celebrate the play-off victory. Half a million people had thronged the streets of Manchester to welcome the United side that a few days before had won the European Cup. We thought it would be inappropriate to parade the play-off trophy. It was, after all, only the first hurdle.

> **Chris Bird:** The *Manchester Evening News*'s City writer was Richard Burgess, who would go on to become head of news at the BBC. The chief sportswriter was Paul Hince, who had played a few

games for City in their championship-winning season in 1967/68 and then played in the lower divisions for Bury, Crewe and Macclesfield. The most important one for me was Peter Spencer, who was the sports editor. I first came across him at the press conference to announce David Bernstein as the new chairman. I went into the kitchen at Maine Road and there's this guy using the internal phone. I said, 'Who are you? Put that phone down.' He turned to me and said: 'Who are you?' It was Peter Spencer. We nearly came to blows. Later, we would get on well. I said to him: 'We are at our lowest ebb, we won't be on the radar of the national press, you are the only conduit for us to City fans in Manchester.' There was no club website, no internet, no social media. There was just the press for getting the message across. Joe Royle was someone who always wanted a good relationship with the local media. He often said to me: 'Always support your local sheriff.'

After we were relegated, *The Times* approached us to do a weekly access-all-areas column about Manchester City in League One. They had done something similar with Barnsley when they had a season in the Premier League. This would be called 'Down Amongst the Dead Men with Manchester City'. The board thought it was a lunatic idea, that we would be exposing ourselves to ridicule. I told them we had nothing to lose, we were rock bottom but we still had an enormous fan base and this was a chance to show that the national media still considered Manchester City to be a good story. And, apart from the *Manchester Evening News*, it was the only regular coverage we would be guaranteed. The series eventually became a book.

Dave Wallace: To me, that season in the Third Division was awful. There was the novelty of going to grounds you had never been to before and there are City fans who will tell you they enjoyed that season more than winning the title, which is something I just cannot believe. Going to Lincoln and losing 2-1 on a wet Tuesday night was no fun. Wycombe doing the double over us was no fun. The worst for me was losing at York. At Bootham Crescent, you had to go behind their kop to go to our stand. We had been selling fanzines before the match and walked across the back of the kop to get to our seats just as they scored. At 1-1 with a few minutes left, we went back out to get ready for selling the fanzine and they scored again. Funnily enough, we didn't sell any. At the end of the play-off final, the feeling was not of exhilaration but of exhaustion and relief that we had done it. I had the same feelings after the European Cup Final against Inter Milan. It was relief that we had won the Treble.

Shaun Goater: I had gone from Rotherham to Bristol City in League One but, when Manchester City came in for me in 1998, I thought: 'This is a huge club.' I agreed without really speaking to anyone. They were a division above but I knew they were struggling; you could see on the football highlights, the fans expressing their frustrations to the players. But I was in a confident mood. I was top goalscorer at Bristol City and I had belief in myself and I thought the move would be good for my career and my form would be good enough to help City back up the table. I went to City with seven games left and they had brought in a psychologist, Bill Beswick, to help motivate the team. You wouldn't have known we'd had a psychologist by some of the results. We were relegated and Bristol City were promoted. We swapped places.

The following season, David Bernstein got us together in the dressing room and gave a talk. Normally, players will switch off if a chairman starts addressing the team but, maybe because I was new to the club, I listened to what he said and he made a real impression. It was an inspiring talk. He said: 'This club has never been in a place like this. All I know is that some of you can become absolute legends by taking us from where we are now to where we belong. If you look around this room, some of you will become legends.' I was eating up every word. It felt as though he was talking to me.

When we went 2-0 down in the play-off final and the ball was going back to the centre circle with a few minutes left, I thought that all of this energy and all of this hard work had been wasted and in vain. When Gillingham took their striker (Carl Asaba) off, he was high-fiving the bench. Then I had a shot and it deflected to Kevin Horlock who struck it into the goal. I was still thinking that this was all in vain because we didn't have enough time. Then they announced five minutes of stoppage time and it provoked this huge roar from the Manchester City fans. I can tell you that roar gave us not just two or three extra yards, it gave us an extra player. I looked around and saw some belief we could get this ball in the goal. I had another shot, it ended up being deflected to Paul Dickov – it was a beautiful deflection because it helped him beat the keeper. Gillingham did well to hold on in extra time but, when it came to penalties, we knew we were going to win. When it happened, the chief emotion was exhaustion. We were absolutely wiped.

Dennis Tueart: Joe Royle had been a pal of mine; we had played for Manchester City together. He had done a great job at Oldham, not so well at Everton, although he had won them the FA Cup. As a manager, you become used to dealing with footballers at a certain level. Joe knew how to handle things where City found themselves. He was backed by Willie Donachie, who was a superb coach, and Asa Hartford. On the board and in the dugout we had City people working for the club and pulling in the same direction.

One of the things we were determined to invest in was the academy and David asked if I could look after it. Jim Cassell ran it brilliantly. He produced 41 first-team footballers for Manchester City, 19 of whom went on to become internationals.

When we got relegated, I said we needed to galvanise everyone on and off the pitch. I said we must bring back Colin Bell, who had been sacked by Francis, give him an ambassadorial role and use him to link up with the supporters.

We had approximately 84 supporters' branches up and down the country. They could fax a form to request that someone from the club visited one of their meetings. We would be open and honest with them. We would not duck the questions. I remember one at Milton Keynes. My offices are in Lymm in Cheshire and I remember leaving the office at five, going home to grab a sandwich and a cup of tea, jumping on the M6 at six o'clock, getting to Milton Keynes at half eight, doing an hour and a half at the meeting and getting home at midnight.

Manchester City captain Roy Paul lifts the 1956 FA Cup. On the day of my bar mitzvah, it only cemented my love for the club.

My uncles and father. From left, Sonny, Joe, Harry, Henry and Cyril.

City fans at Stoke, facing the reality of relegation to the third tier of English football.

Queen Elizabeth studying a model of the City of Manchester Stadium.

Shaun Goater was one of the key players in my time as chairman.

Andy Morrison lifts perhaps the most important trophy in Manchester City's history.

The overwhelming feeling after the play-off final was one of relief.

Signing the agreement for the new stadium on the pitch at Maine Road with council leader, Richard Leese, and chief executive, Howard Bernstein.

Relaxing with Joe Royle and our wives.

Keeper Nicky Weaver carried aloft after the final home game of the 1999/2000 season.

Nothing encapsulates the feeling of promotion more than this photo of Joe Royle hugging Mark Kennedy.

City fans flood on to the pitch at Ewood Park as City regain the Premier League.

Maine Road, our home since 1923, prepares for its final bow ...

... while the arena that was to become the symbol of a new club takes shape.

Chris Bird and I inspect progress at the City of Manchester Stadium.

All smiles from Joe Royle and me as City return to the Premier League at Charlton. The 4-0 defeat was a sign of things to come.

We would take players, directors, people from the commercial and marketing departments to listen to them. We wanted to show our supporters what we were doing.

We had to let the players understand where we were. I said to David, and Joe Royle supported me, that you have got to talk to the players. They knew we were in trouble; they probably knew that finances were tight. I suggested with David and Joe's support that we should only pay them bonuses if we were in the top six at the end of the month. David was very nervous about doing this but we went to see the players' committee with Joe in his office at Platt Lane. We needed them to know where we were.

If we had not beaten Gillingham in the play-offs, I don't know where the club would have been. We would probably have spent years drifting between the Second and Third Divisions. There would have been a fire sale – either of players or of their contracts. In football, momentum is a massive thing and mostly it is an emotional thing. The play-offs lifted everyone; in the dressing room, in the boardroom and in the stands of Maine Road. The momentum carried us through the following season and into the Premier League.

Alistair Mackintosh: I was in London about to take up a job with *The Economist*, not as a journalist but on the accounting and business side of the magazine. I had been an accountant at Price Waterhouse and had joined Sony and had accepted a job on *The Economist.* I had had seven interviews for that job and, on the day I got the letter informing me that I'd been appointed, David contacted me offering an interview about a post as Manchester City's financial controller. It was for way less money than *The Economist* was offering but I was excited about it straight away.

I had been born in Manchester in Wythenshawe Hospital; my mum had worked in the Christie (Manchester's leading cancer hospital). I was 28 when I came up to Manchester City. It was a real culture shock because Sony was very IT-based and Manchester City was the complete opposite, people were still hand-writing journals to create the most basic financial statements. On my first day, I had to persuade one of the accountants, Andy Hardman, not to resign. He is still at the club as head of football administration. At the play-off final, when it was 2-0 to Gillingham, I looked around at all the Manchester City staff who had come down to Wembley by bus to watch the game and I thought: 'Unless things change pretty quickly, I'm probably going to have to make all of these people redundant.'

Money

BEFORE MANCHESTER City won promotion in the most dramatic way possible, I was made an offer, which had I accepted it, would have seen me hanged from a lamppost outside Maine Road. It would have been a punishment I would have thoroughly deserved.

The offer came from Wimbledon. They wanted to merge with Manchester City to create a new club that would play its fixtures at Maine Road. Wimbledon had been homeless since selling Plough Lane in 1991 and were growing tired of ground-sharing with Crystal Palace. In 1996, they had tried and failed to move to Dublin, which would have involved building a new stadium at a cost of £100m and paying every League of Ireland club £250,000. Wimbledon would then be able to directly tap into the huge Irish support for Premier League football. The idea dissolved in the face of opposition from the Football Association of Ireland and FIFA.

Their chairman, Sam Hammam, having seen his ambitions frustrated, sold his majority stake in the club to a Norwegian consortium, who continued to explore avenues to relocate. If they could not go to Dublin, then perhaps Manchester was an option? Their plan was to merge with Manchester City and form a single club. They would get our fanbase – who would almost certainly have rebelled against the idea – and a ground, first at Maine Road and then at the new City of Manchester Stadium. We would get their players, who in 1999 had just reached the semi-finals of the League and the FA Cups. We would also get their place in the Premier League without having to worry about winning promotion ourselves.

Because the idea was never more than an exploratory approach – I turned Wimbledon down flat – I can only surmise how the plan might have worked. We may have ended up being called 'Manchester City Dons' much as Milton Keynes Dons emerged a few years later. I imagine 'Manchester City Dons' would have suffered the same fate as 'Thames Valley Royals', the club Robert Maxwell planned to create through a merger of Oxford United and Reading in 1983. Maxwell owned Oxford and had a 19 per cent stake in Reading but his proposals foundered on a wave of supporter protest and legal challenges.

I can only speculate, but it is unlikely any merger would have been a quick process and time was not on Wimbledon's side. By May 2000, we had regained our place in the Premier League and they had been relegated. Their greatest bargaining chip was gone, never to return.

Just after watching Manchester City's promotion at Wembley, I received an intriguing message that was to have rather more substance than the idea floated by Wimbledon. Would I be prepared to come to Glasgow and meet with the Rangers chairman, David Murray? I said 'Yes'. Since taking over at Ibrox in 1988, Murray had turned Rangers into the dominant force in Scottish football with a turnover that bore comparison with some leading Premier League clubs. When I met him, he told me he wanted to buy Manchester City. Or at least a part of it.

The previous summer had seen Rangers coming to terms with the fact that they were no longer champions of Scotland. Since they had been Scottish champions every year since Murray's takeover, this did not seem like much of a crisis when seen from Maine Road. However, at Ibrox it was seen as a slap in the face. Murray was a man used to overcoming adversity. In 1976, he had lost both legs in a car crash and, more recently, his wife had succumbed to cancer.

It has been my experience that people who have overcome great personal loss are especially driven to succeed in business and this seems to have been the case with David.

Epitomised by his comment that 'for every five pounds Celtic spend, Rangers will spend ten', Murray ordered an expansive financial response. Dick Advocaat, who had managed Holland in the 1994 World Cup, was hired to replace Walter Smith, who had joined Everton. Advocaat was Rangers' first foreign manager. The Scottish transfer record was broken to take the Russian winger, Andrei Kanchelskis, from Fiorentina. They won back the league title at the first attempt. The move to buy into Manchester City was part of this expansionist programme. When Rangers collapsed into administration and then liquidation in 2012, this heavy spending was deemed to be one of the root causes.

For football purposes, England and Scotland are treated as entirely separate countries, so there would have been no barrier to the sale. Manchester City would have become a feeder club for Rangers. We would have received some of their fringe players, plus a financial investment. Rangers would have had a director on the board.

The way Manchester City was structured meant you did not have to buy all of the club to control it. In the summer of 1999, 39 per cent of the club's shares were in the names of Stephen Boler, Peter Swales and Francis Lee. The first two were dead – Swales had died of a heart attack just before City's relegation from the Premier League in 1996 – and their shares were in family trusts. Francis was thought to be permanently in the background. Rangers would target these shares.

On 28 June, I received a letter detailing Murray's plans. Rangers would put £17.5m into Manchester City; £12m would be available for Joe Royle to spend on the team and £2 million would pay off loans to John Wardle and David Makin. 'The estimate of £12m to strengthen the current playing squad is made on the assumption that Manchester City will stay in Division One (the second tier) for two seasons. We would not expect this amount to be spent in full in the 1999/2000 season.'

Rangers would invest £9.5m from their own funds. A further £5m would come from a loan, while the final £3m would be in the form of an additional overdraft facility with the Co-op Bank. One of the questions they wanted to examine was how well we could repay debt. Once the dust had settled, Rangers would own 39 per cent of the club. The only shareholders who came close to their proposed stake were Makin and Wardle with 28 per cent. Murray would have bought effective control of Manchester City for £17.5m – some of which would be debt we would be responsible for.

I was highly sceptical about Rangers' approach but it needed to be addressed properly and professionally. The man I tasked with examining this document was Peter Rickitt, an extraordinary, flamboyant corporate financial adviser based in Manchester. He was so big he could barely squeeze through my office door and could empty a bottle of Bollinger champagne with giddying speed. He had a sharp eye and he was not impressed by the offer coming from Glasgow. City would be liable for £1.45m in interest payments a year. He faxed me in Italy, where I was on holiday, with his assessment of the offer. He ended the fax with the comment: 'Do you really need the players that much!?'

We did not. At a board meeting the following month, we made it clear to Joe Royle that the priority was to reduce the still-bloated size of the playing staff and the only substantial purchase Joe had made that summer was to pay Wimbledon £1.6m for their Irish winger, Mark Kennedy. He did not feel the squad needed significant adjustments. Money was still, however, an issue at Maine Road. A tie-up with the Chicago-based Bank One to launch a Manchester City credit card earned us £500,000. Three months later came a deal that would earn us very much more than that. In April 1999, BSkyB had seen its nine-month campaign to buy Manchester United – which had the support of the board at Old Trafford – fall foul of the Monopolies and Mergers Commission. That had not ended the broadcaster's interest in other football clubs as an investment opportunity and, in November, they made a £7.5m investment in Manchester City that would give them 9.9 per cent of the club. They would pay a further £2m to become City's media agent. Internally, there would be a rights issue while David Makin and John Wardle, who stepped up to become deputy chairman, agreed to convert their £4.8m of loans into shares that had the effect of reducing the club's debt and the interest we paid on it. The total package was worth £20m to Manchester City. The front-page headline in the *Manchester Evening News* read: 'Bonanza For Blues'.

The paper described us as 'Division One kings' and on the day it appeared – 5 November 1999 – we were top of Division One, leading Charlton by six points. For a newly promoted club, which had not made big investments in players, our progress had been astonishingly smooth.

Although the season had begun with a 1-0 defeat at home to Wolverhampton Wanderers, we won our next eight games at Maine Road, putting six past Sheffield United and four past Portsmouth. Victories over clubs such as Nottingham Forest, Crystal Palace and Blackburn only increased our credibility. The campaign finished at Maine Road with a 1-0 win over Birmingham that sparked a pitch invasion by fans who thought the win was enough to see us promoted. However, if Ipswich beat Charlton, who were already up, the following day, the race for automatic promotion would go to the final round of matches. Sure enough, Ipswich won 3-1 at The Valley.

Sunday, 7 May 2000, is not a date with the same resonance as 30 May 1999 in the blue half of Manchester, but the match was almost as extraordinary. Again, we did not wear sky blue but the red-and-black 'AC Milan' shirts. We were two points ahead of Ipswich and, to go up, we needed only a draw at Blackburn. If we lost and Ipswich won, we would be denied. They were at home to Walsall, who were in the relegation zone. We were away to a team that five years before had been champions of England.

There were 15,000 City fans at Ewood Park, most inside the stadium, some watching bare-chested in the sunshine on the grassy slopes above the ground. Throughout the match, sky blue and white balloons drifted down on to the pitch – a pitch which, for an hour, was the scene of one of our limpest performances of the season. Not only did Matt Jansen open the scoring for Graeme Souness's side, but Blackburn also hit the frame of the goal four times. Joe was sitting beside me in the directors' box. He had been unwell the previous night but, when Jansen scored, our manager betrayed no emotion. At Portman Road, Ipswich were drawing with Walsall but they would win easily enough.

Joe was very calm in the dressing room during the interval and once Shaun Goater equalised at the far post with his 29th goal of the season, the floodgates opened. Manchester City ran out 4-1 winners. There is a wonderful photograph of Mark Kennedy, having scored City's second, running towards the manager. Joe's arms are outstretched, his tie loosened, he is grinning broadly. It encapsulated in a single image the transformation that had come over the club.

Because I did not want to tempt fate, I had not organised any celebrations but, as soon as we were up, I asked Layachi Bouskouchi to contact the Midland Hotel in Manchester and organise a party that evening. Layachi was a remarkable man. He was from Tangiers, ran a newsagents' in Chorlton and knew everyone at Manchester City. He was the club 'fixer'. He got things done. 'This time,' I told Layachi, 'we will drink champagne.'

Layachi did his work. When we arrived, two hours later, the Midland's restaurant had been transformed with a pyramid of champagne bottles in the middle. During the evening, hundreds of fans gathered outside the hotel singing choruses of 'Blue Moon', prompting the players to gather on the hotel balcony to applaud the supporters. When it was time to go, a policeman told me not to leave via the main entrance as it would cause a disturbance. It was rare for any football club chairman to be confronted by crowds expressing only love.

The Bubbles Burst

MANCHESTER CITY'S journey from the first to the third tier of English football and back again had been giddyingly swift. City were not the only club that would be relegated from the Premier League, drop into what is now League One, and return to the top flight, but we were the first to do so and ours would be the quickest comeback. Other big clubs went down two divisions and came back up. However, it took Southampton and Norwich seven years, Leeds 16 years and Nottingham Forest 23. Some clubs, like Coventry, Sheffield Wednesday and Sunderland have, at the time of writing, still to complete the journey.

In 1996, Peter Reid had taken Sunderland into the Premier League a year after the club had narrowly avoided relegation to the third tier. They were not ready for it. Sunderland had not completed the move from Roker Park to a new stadium and the squad required a major upgrade.

Funds were tight. Twelve months later, they would be relegated. When asked if they had gone up too soon, the Sunderland chairman, Bob Murray, replied there was never a bad time to be promoted. I would agree with Bob. You cannot pick and choose your promotions.

We returned to a Premier League which was growing apace but which was nothing like the scale it had reached when Southampton earned more than £100m for finishing bottom in 2023. To run a big Premier League club now, you would need to have the operation run by a number of specialists. You could not try to oversee the workings of the whole club as I had to do in 2000. It was a delicate balancing act. I had always been acutely aware that any ambitious, developing organisation needed solid foundations. Yet, if we were over-cautious, we ran the risk of allowing the achievements of the last two seasons to slip away.

In many ways, being in the Premier League made things easier. Corporate hospitality and sponsorship were simpler to sell. It was soon evident Maine Road was not big enough for our supporters' needs. The biggest change was the make-up of our playing staff and the person who had to adapt the most was Joe Royle. He had managed in the Premier League with Everton, but the Premier League had changed significantly since he left Goodison Park in March 1997. Arsène Wenger had begun to revolutionise the way footballers were trained, how they were recruited and how they lived their lives off the pitch. Footballers were coming to the Premier League from more diverse backgrounds. It was a rapidly changing environment.

Some managers, like Sir Alex Ferguson, Roy Hodgson and Sir Bobby Robson, adapted. However, the old school ways of bonding over boozy nights out in Chinese restaurants, a tactic Howard Kendall had used successfully at Everton, or ruling with an iron fist like Graeme Souness were on their way out. In 2003, Peter Reid went to manage Leeds. He found he could not order around the new breed of players, all of whom were millionaires and some of whom had played in the Champions League, in the way he had done at Sunderland or Manchester City. The balance of power in the dressing room had changed. In retrospect, I do not feel Royle had the flexibility to adapt to this rapidly changing environment.

However, in the summer of 2000, Joe carried with him an enormous amount of goodwill and respect. He had our complete confidence. His signings hitherto had been good – Shaun Goater, Andy Morrison and Nicky Weaver all had

a decisive impact on Manchester City's progress. Joe spe most of the early part of the close season attempting to si Ugo Ehiogu from Aston Villa. The centre-half went Middlesbrough for £7m.

Two players he did bring to Maine Road stirred re excitement. We knew George Weah was coming to the en of his career. He had been World Player of the Year in 199 but he was now over 30 and his contract with AC Mila would not be renewed. He had spent part of the previous season on loan at Chelsea and had scored on his debut against Tottenham. He would be available for £100,000 paid to his agent, Ian Anderson. We thought Weah had enough left in him to warrant a transfer. Joe thought he could have a significant role as an impact player from the bench.

The other signing that generated back-page headlines in the national media was that of Paulo Wanchope, a gangly, loose-limbed centre-forward from Costa Rica who had once played basketball in the United States. In April 1997, when playing for Derby, Wanchope had slalomed through the Manchester United defence at Old Trafford to score one of the Premier League's great goals.

Wanchope was now with West Ham. I approached Paul Aldridge, the managing director at Upton Park, and agreed a

fee of £3.65m – although nobody at Upton Park appeared to have informed the player. We agreed that Paulo would come to Manchester to discuss personal terms. It was a meeting Wanchope did not make. Dennis Tueart, Bernard Halford and I found ourselves speaking only to his agent, Dennis Roach. He told us Paulo was reluctant to leave London and also that Bradford were interested in the player. The negotiations lasted a number of days during which Roach asked for £250,000 for his services. He would then act on Manchester City's behalf to make sure the transfer was completed.

When we pointed out that Roach was Wanchope's agent and that he could hardly act for both parties in the transfer, he suggested that, if Paulo was due a signing-on fee of £500,000, he could be given half of that. We said 'No'. The way Dennis Roach conducted himself in these talks infuriated Joe Royle, who told Roach that he was acting in a wholly unprofessional manner. Joe never believed the talk that Bradford might be an alternative destination to Manchester City.

What especially upset Joe was the fact that our main summer signing was not available for our opening game of the season, at Charlton. That the match was lost, 4-0, only increased our anger. Paulo had been on international

duty with Costa Rica but he should have arrived back in England in time to travel to London. The former Arsenal player, Bob McNab, who was now working in Los Angeles and represented Paulo in the United States, told me of the confusion that surrounded the transfer in a letter I received in November.

McNab told me that it was only when arriving back in England that Wanchope learnt he had been sold. He was told he could go to either Bradford or Manchester City. McNab wrote: 'One day later, Paulo called me to inform me of the situation. I told him he must be courteous to Bradford City but under no circumstances should he go there, whatever they were prepared to pay, and that Manchester City would be a good club to consider. Paulo was extremely upset and disappointed that West Ham had sold him.'

A few days later, McNab received a 'frantic' call from Roach saying that he could not get hold of Wanchope. McNab spoke to the player, who did not want to speak to Roach. McNab added: 'I think it's fair to confirm that, at the time, Paulo was hurt, embarrassed, confused and extremely upset with West Ham and more interested in damaging them than getting on with what was in his own best interests. I should also reiterate that in the two conversations

I had with Mr Roach he was beside himself with worry that Paulo would lose the Manchester offer if Paulo did not speed things up.'

Wanchope did arrive in time for the first home game of the season, on Wednesday, 23 August, against Sunderland. He scored the opening goal, played through by George Weah, after two minutes, laid on the second for Alf-Inge Haaland, and finished with a hat-trick in a 4-2 victory.

The experiment with Weah did not last long. He had started the first three games of the season – the third was a 2-1 defeat at home to Coventry – but Joe concluded he lacked the stamina for a full 90 minutes. He would either come off the bench or start but be substituted in the second half. However, after both he and Paulo put in a desultory performance in a 1-0 defeat to Newcastle at the end of September, there was a dressing-room row with the manager. Paul Dickov led the attack in the next two games, back-to-back victories against Bradford and Southampton which pushed City into tenth place.

It was then that we were informed that Weah no longer wished to play for Manchester City. There was a meeting with Weah, his agent, Ian Anderson, Dennis Tueart, Joe

Royle and Chris Bird. Chris thought our relationship with Weah was worth saving but Joe did not. His contract was terminated for a fee of £500,000. He arranged a transfer to Olympique Marseille and then issued a statement.

In it, Weah said: 'I was made to feel old and of no use to the club. I felt I was being used as publicity to attract other players.' Before leaving for France, Weah, who owned a boot factory in Italy, gave away all his brightly coloured boots and training tops to the rest of the Manchester City squad, who took them as souvenirs. Shaun Goater remembered the one-time World Footballer of the Year and future president of Liberia as 'a man without any airs or graces; a normal guy who was ready to pass on advice to the youngsters and blend in as best he could'. Shaun thought the presence of Weah might have encouraged other foreign footballers to come to the club. Tueart suggested the fact that Weah, Wanchope, Steve Howey and Laurent Charvet – the latter two had been signed from Newcastle – were on more money than the men who had won Manchester City promotion sowed discord in the dressing room. It was an argument Royle had some sympathy with. However, in his memoirs, Richard Edghill, the man who had scored the winning penalty in the play-off final, wrote that wages were not an issue when he and some others from that day at Wembley found themselves in the Premier League.

Edghill wrote: 'The club had made it clear they were breaking the existing wage structure when they sanctioned the deal to bring George to the club. There was a core of us who had escorted the club through the divisions and were on a certain level of wages. We knew the next group were coming in on much more but, to us, it didn't really matter that much. We weren't bothered what they were on because we knew it was a completely different level of salary – a level we could not have achieved through agent negotiation anyway.'

Joe thought Weah exerted considerable influence on Wanchope and that his departure unsettled the Costa Rican. At Stamford Bridge, during a 2-1 defeat by Chelsea in December, there was a physical confrontation between the manager and his centre-forward during the interval. When informed that he was being substituted for Dickov, Wanchope tried to attack Joe and only the intervention of other players prevented a fist fight. The pressure was intense. This was City's sixth straight defeat in the league – including three trips to London that had seen us lose to Arsenal, West Ham and now Chelsea by a combined score of 11-2. In that time, Manchester City had fallen from 10th to 16th and were now just two points clear of a relegation place.

On the Monday, player and manager met at Platt Lane. Joe recalled the encounter in his autobiography: 'There was something disturbing about the indifference, bordering on arrogance, that emanated from him as I spoke. Paulo barely said a word during what was, in effect, a one-way conversation and I was left with the deepening conviction that there was an unbridgeable gap between us.'

Joe then told me that he wanted to put Wanchope on the transfer list. I rang Dennis Tueart, who was at Liverpool Airport waiting for a plane for a business trip to Barcelona. Dennis was astonished by the decision because the previous day Joe had told him he wanted to let the incident settle before we decided on any action. Dennis's first concern was that, if Wanchope were transfer-listed, he would be entitled to the whole of his £500,000 signing-on fee. If he asked to leave, we could negotiate a compromise figure.

Wanchope remained in the starting line-up. He scored the opening goal of the next game – a 5-0 thrashing of Everton – and scored again in a 2-2 draw at Aston Villa. He was a regular member of the team until he suffered a knee injury in an FA Cup fourth-round victory over Coventry on 27 January. It was then that his agent, Dennis Roach, became involved. On 8 February he wrote to Joe.

'Paulo has a connection in Barcelona with the assistant coach of the Costa Rican national team. Since he is recovering from his knee operation, would it be possible for him to go over to Spain, where the weather is warm and he would have the full facilities he needs to continue his return to fitness? You are aware that he is a very good trainer and very dedicated and professional. He feels it would do him a great deal of good to get a break from our winter.

'He will be well looked after by the Barcelona people and there would be direct contact numbers to speak with him as you wish. In respect of costs, it would represent an air fare and a hotel bill. There would be no further charges and you could discuss who would pay this with Paulo direct.'

Joe refused permission for Paulo to travel to Spain. The next day, Roach wrote to me. After informing me he had just returned from 'a well-deserved holiday to South Africa', Roach stated Paulo did not want to leave Manchester City, that his mother and girlfriend had just come up to Manchester to live with him and that he was in year one of a four-year contract. He attached an article from the *Manchester Evening News* before a League Cup quarter-final against Ipswich in which Joe talked about the striker in fulsome terms. The fixture was after the incident at Stamford Bridge – which demonstrated Joe was not prepared to criticise his player in public. Roach concluded his letter by wondering how this relationship could have deteriorated so quickly.

A few days later, Roach wrote to me again, complaining that after Wanchope had undergone his knee operation, nobody from the club was there to pick him up. When Paulo went to the David Lloyd health club in Cheadle to begin his rehabilitation, he was told his membership had been cancelled. I told his agent I would look into it.

I was also looking into something else, something that would not ordinarily concern the chairman of a Premier League club. It was a bar bill. The Christmas fixture list has always been seen from abroad as an exhausting, peculiarly English tradition but, even by our standards, it had been a punitive set of matches. On 23 December, we travelled to Sunderland, where we lost 1-0 in flurries of snow. On Boxing Day, we had a goalless draw with Derby at Maine Road. On Saturday, 30 December, Charlton beat us 4-1 at Maine Road. Two days later, on New Year's Day, we would play Coventry at Highfield Road. We would go there second from bottom of the Premier League. Coventry were two places and one point above us. It was a critical fixture.

On New Year's Eve, the team stayed overnight at the Forest of Arden hotel, near Birmingham Airport. They celebrated the New Year in style. According to the bills the hotel submitted for payment, less than 24 hours before the Coventry game, the Manchester City management team and backroom staff purchased: 49 whiskies or Southern Comforts, 56 vodkas, 61 gins, 24 rums, 19 Baileys, 20 brandies, nine schnapps, 33 beers or lagers, four ciders, three bottles of wine, ten glasses of champagne, one bottle of Moet et Chandon and three pina coladas. They also ordered 11 Cuban cigars. The tab was closed at 1.37am. Paulo Wanchope ordered an apple pudding to be sent to his room at half-past eight. He scored City's goal in a 1-1 draw. The bills were from just two tables, 103 and 111, and were signed for by Joe or by Les Chapman, the kit man, and each had the same tip of £50.

Marc Edworthy, who had not scored in four years, was responsible for Coventry's equaliser with a hopeful punt that somehow squirmed underneath Nicky Weaver's body. The television commentary described City's play as 'a shambles' in the closing moments. Nevertheless, we had played much better than we had against Charlton.

Joe vehemently contested the bills from the Forest of Arden, claiming that multiple tables simply put their tabs on the Manchester City account and that had he and his staff really drunk that amount, none of them would have made it to Highfield Road. I was not aware of the scale of the drinking at the club and perhaps I should have been. However, I lived in London and this was an age before camera phones and social media recorded the movements of every professional footballer.

Richard Dunne, a centre-half we had signed from Everton for £3m, was fined for unauthorised drinking several times by Joe Royle and this was mentioned in board meetings. There were also incidents when, in the spring of 2000 and again a year later, the squad went abroad for warm-weather training. In 2000, Royle told the media a trip to Lanzarote would 'freshen up the minds as well as the bodies'. One highlight was the sight of Jeff Whitley, who would later receive treatment for alcoholism, and Mark Kennedy turning up to a team meeting in sombreros and sarongs and smoking cigars. Both were drunk. Nothing much was made of the incident because Manchester City were on their way to promotion.

In 2001, with the club threatened by relegation, Joe organised another trip, this time to the Costa del Sol. Andrei Kanchelskis, whom we had signed on loan from Glasgow Rangers, recalled seeing Steve Howey lying on his bed surrounded by bottles of beer. Kanchelskis thought there was very little training and that City would have been better off staying at Carrington. A damaging pattern of behaviour was becoming apparent that would have serious repercussions.

Shaun Goater: It was that 1999/2000 promotion season that I first became aware of the 'Feed the Goat' chants. Initially, I thought it was for another player because I was so tuned into the game and didn't hear it properly. When I got back into the dressing room, the lads were saying: 'They are singing for you.' George Weah arrived when I was recovering from an injury. I was a student of the game and I always wanted to watch and learn from the best players. George would make runs but our players weren't quite good enough to find him. It gave me confidence because I'd be thinking that

I had been making some of those same runs and the passes hadn't found me either and George had won the Ballon d'Or and won the European Cup with AC Milan. He let me know that the runs I was making were the right ones.

Chris Bird: We were due to play Ipswich in a League Cup tie in December 2000 but there was torrential rain over Manchester. I didn't have enough groundstaff and we didn't even have covers. I rang the groundsman at United and asked if we could borrow some of their groundstaff and their covers. They sent them over. The game went on but was abandoned at half-time with City leading 2-0 – we would lose the rearranged match 2-1. I went up to the chairman's suite to tell them and Alex Ferguson was thcrc. If United didn't have a game, he would come to Maine Road. I stood there in my sodden club suit to announce it to everyone and, as I walked away, Fergie said: 'Your groundsman's young.' I had never met Fergie before and wouldn't encounter him again until four years later when they announced Wayne Rooney's signing. I'd left City by then but was doing some work for Bet Fred, who were one of Manchester United's sponsors. Fergie walked up and said: 'Who let Manchester City's groundsman in?' It shows one of Alex Ferguson's greatest attributes, his phenomenal memory.

Anatomy of a Tackle

THERE WAS not much to celebrate as 2000 turned into 2001. Manchester City did not win a league match until 24 February, when Shaun Goater's goal gave us a win at Newcastle. It was not enough to move us out of the relegation zone. For 140 days between December and April we did not win a league game at Maine Road. On 21 April, we would face Manchester United at Old Trafford. United were 16 points clear of Arsenal. A victory would see them win the title, which would be their third in a row.

Our relations with our neighbours were polite but necessarily distant. You could not be seen to be fraternising with the enemy. It was a source of great pride to me that our derbies with Bury and Stockport had given way to the traditional ones against Manchester United. That season, at Euston, I had sat down in a train carriage opposite a man, his face hidden behind a newspaper. When the paper was put down, the face revealed itself to be Sir Alex Ferguson. We chatted amicably enough for two hours on the journey to Manchester. It was fascinating to have the opportunity to spend time with the greatest manager in British football.

Despite all that was riding on the derby, a lot of the conversation at the two training grounds, which were now a mile apart at Carrington, concerned how Roy Keane, the Manchester United captain, would deal with Alf-Inge Haaland. In September 1997, Haaland had been playing for Leeds against Manchester United at Elland Road. His manager, David O'Leary, had given him the task of marking Keane out of the game, something he had done with great success.

Keane, who had been drinking into the small hours of Thursday morning, was having, by his own account, 'a bloody awful' match on the Saturday. Leeds were leading 1-0, Keane lunged at Haaland to make a tackle, his studs became caught in the turf and he could hear the cruciate ligament snap in his knee. Haaland told him to 'get up and stop faking it'. Keane did not play again for the rest of the season. As the derby approached, Steve Howey recalled: 'It was just boiling up and boiling up. Everyone knew Keane was going to do it. It was just a case of when.'

Keane said he had waited more than three years to settle his score with Haaland. There had been a verbal encounter between the two men in the first derby of the season, at Maine Road in November. United had won the game with a David Beckham free kick. Now, with four minutes remaining of the Old Trafford match – in a game that Keane remarked that City were up for but United were not – he launched himself at Haaland in what I can only describe as a premeditated assault. Alfie anticipated the tackle and tried to turn and ride it. If he had kept both feet planted on the ground, Keane would have broken his leg.

As it was, he finished the match, which was drawn 1-1, and travelled to Norway for a friendly against Bulgaria. He did not complete the game. He played in City's 1-0 win over West Ham on 28 April but came off after 67 minutes. In both cases, the cause was severe pain in his knee.

I have never forgiven Keane for what was an assault. Even now, I refuse to watch him as a television pundit. On the Monday after the derby, I wrote to the FA:

'Our captain, Alf-Inge Haaland, was subject to a cynical, vicious and career-threatening foul by the Manchester United captain Roy Keane. His remarks to our player, as he lay on the ground, indicated that this action was premeditated and, in effect, settling a vendetta. The referee acted quite properly in showing Keane a red card. However, we believe that the nature of this foul, at a volatile derby match with all the obvious crowd implications, in front of a worldwide TV audience, takes this incident out of the ordinary. We are looking to the FA to act appropriately and ensure that the punishment fits the crime.'

The FA stated that it would require a formal statement of complaint from Alfie Haaland. I replied on 29 May:

'Neither Mr Haaland nor ourselves wishes to make a formal statement of complaint as we are not looking to make difficulties between our two clubs. However, as stated in my previous letter, the evidence is quite clear and was seen by tens of millions of people and publicised in the press. We would look to the FA to deal with this matter and protect the good name of football. There is little else we can say except that this matter requires a practical and not a legalistic approach.'

The FA fined Keane £5,000 and banned him for three games, which was a standard penalty for a straight red card. Alfie would start only one more game for Manchester City before injury finished his career. It was meniscal tears in his knees, particularly the left one, that forced the decision.

The left knee, which had been scanned four days before, had troubled him for several months and had been strapped during the derby. Keane had targeted Alfie's right knee. I was, however, determined to discover whether Keane's tackle had exacerbated the prognosis. There was medical evidence that the blow to the right knee had damaged the left as Alfie turned to ride the tackle.

In September 2002, after the publication of Keane's autobiography in which he confessed that the tackle had been premeditated, I and the club lawyer, Bryan Bodek, met with a barrister, Brian Langstaff QC, to see if we or Haaland could sue the Manchester United captain for damages. Langstaff told us that Haaland had a case for assault. Haaland told us that, before the game, Manchester United's Norwegian players, Ole Gunnar Solskjaer and Henning Berg, had warned him that Keane had been talking in the dressing room about what he intended to do. As Haaland lay on the floor in the wake of the challenge, Keane told him: 'I have waited a long time for this.'

Our main case study was Watson v Gray. It centred on a match between Bradford and Huddersfield in February 1997. Gordon Watson, a striker who had just joined Bradford from Southampton for a club record figure of £575,000, had his leg broken in two places by a two-footed tackle from Kevin Gray. Watson and Bradford sued Gray and Huddersfield on the grounds that the tackle, which Jimmy Hill called the worst he had seen in 50 years in football and which was punished with just a yellow card, had cost Watson 18 months of his career and a potential £30,000 in goalscoring bonuses.

The High Court in Leeds ruled that Gray knew he was taking a risk when he launched into a tackle. In May 1999, the month Bradford were promoted to the Premier League, Watson was awarded £909,143, based on loss of earnings and loss of future earnings. After the tackle, Watson played just 80 more minutes for Bradford City. Haaland had a contract with Manchester City that ran until 2005. He was unable to fulfil the last three years of it. At that time, we had paid him a basic salary of £779,000 a year.

Brian Langstaff thought it unlikely Manchester United would want to put Keane into the witness box 'unless they want to put forward his image as a hardman'. United might be tempted to settle out of court. If it came to court, they could argue Haaland already had a meniscal tear and degenerative arthritis in his left knee which would have curtailed his career anyway. If they lost, United might have to pay only for the acceleration of the ending of Haaland's career.

As Langstaff put it: 'You knock someone over in your car and you are to blame. The victim's leg has to be amputated as a result and therefore you could be held liable for a lot of damages. However, it then emerges that, unknown to you, there was a cancer in his leg which would have resulted in the amputation of the leg within three years. What would the defendant have to pay? The defendant would have to pay the difference between what would have been and what actually happened.'

He said a claim from Manchester City that Haaland's injury had deprived us of his services for our last three games and contributed to our relegation was very unlikely to succeed. 'Judges are very unlikely to second guess the results of football matches,' he said.

Alfie was insured for £1m. However, as Bryan Bodek pointed out: 'For this policy to come into being, there needs to be an actual incident involving the player which leads to this permanent disablement. A degenerative condition such as arthritis is unlikely to be covered. We have no insurance policy to cover lost wages.' Haaland's salary was £15,000 per week plus an appearance fee of £7,500. For the last three years of his contract, which his knees would not let him fulfil, that fee would have risen to £10,000.

The following month, the matter was settled by a fax from Andrew Williams, a consultant at the Chelsea and Westminster Hospital who had been asked to analyse Alfie's medical records and the various scans on his knees.

Williams wrote that there was 'unarguable evidence' that the player's knee was damaged before the tackle. We might have been able to claim that Keane's challenge precipitated a chain of events that accelerated the inevitable but Williams concluded his report with: 'I feel Mr Haaland has a very weak case on medical grounds. Mr Keane would have a robust case.' Reluctantly, I decided I had no option but to discontinue proceedings.

There was, however, a justice of sorts. Keane's autobiography led to charges by the FA that he had deliberately set out to injure a fellow professional and that, by writing about it, he had profited from the incident – Penguin Books is believed to have paid the Irishman £1.4m for his memoirs. On 16 October, he arrived with Manchester United's lawyer, Maurice Watkins, for a hearing at Bolton's Reebok Stadium.

Sir Alex Ferguson, naturally, claimed there was no case for his captain to answer. 'I think there has been a going and toing between these players over the years, particularly from Haaland,' he said. 'He's had plenty to say. Every time we played them, he made comments about Roy in the papers but we didn't complain.'

The FA believed there was a case and pursued it vigorously. Their lawyer, a QC called Jim Sturman, was brutally effective. 'He was brilliant,' Keane recalled in the second volume of his autobiography. 'He had me on toast.' The key moment came when Keane's ghostwriter, Eamon Dunphy, was asked to give evidence. Sturman asked him: 'Do you think Mr Keane intentionally went to injure his fellow professional, Mr Haaland?'

Dunphy replied: 'Without a doubt.' Keane was fined £150,000 – which was more than three times the previous record fine the FA had imposed on a player – and banned for five matches.

The cost to Alfie was rather greater. We consulted John Bergfield, a knee specialist based in Cleveland, Ohio. His prognosis was that it was unlikely Haaland would ever play football at his former level. Alfie was also seen by an orthopaedic specialist in Norway. Fluid was drained from the knee but this failed to improve it and, on 13 February 2003, I told Alfie that we would be giving him six months' notice that his contract would be terminated. He was 30 years old.

In his second autobiography, published in 2015, Keane wrote how passive Haaland's team-mates had been in the seconds after the tackle: 'Looking back, I'm disappointed in the other Manchester City players. They didn't jump in to defend their team-mate.' I like to think that behind the scenes we did everything we could to help Alfie after one of the most notorious challenges in the history of the Premier League.

A Parting of the Ways

MY RELATIONSHIP with Joe Royle was one of the closest of my professional life. We would speak almost every day and he was a man for whom I had great respect. However, as the season reached its climax, it was clear he was out of sorts and under great stress. His movement had been impaired by a hip operation, which caused him constant pain. In the New Year, I went to see him in Ormskirk, just to check that he was all right.

On 11 April, we played a night match at home to Arsenal, who were four up inside 36 minutes. We had been completely outclassed and humiliated on our own pitch by a side that started without Thierry Henry and Patrick Vieira.

Afterwards, Joe told me that, standing in the tunnel at Maine Road before the match, he felt like he was in the Land of the Giants. The Arsenal team was so much bigger and more physically impressive than Manchester City's. He then added, as an aside: 'The press are after me.'

I was never one to avoid the media but this time I did. I felt it was important to support Joe in any way I could and, if I could do it only through silence, then I would. Manchester City were five points from safety with five games left and without a home win since December. The only question any journalist would want to ask me was whether the board still had faith in Joe. To answer 'No' would make the manager's position untenable. 'Yes' was the only possible response – but to answer 'Yes' would not be accurate because my confidence in Joe was fraying. For the only time as chairman, I hid. After the match, I shut myself away in the Midland Hotel and refused to take any calls.

In hindsight, the question must be whether we showed too much faith in Joe. Had we sacked him with seven or eight games remaining, would Manchester City have survived?

However, Joe had taken us from the third tier of English football to the Premier League and sacking your manager late on is a questionable survival technique. In the last months of the 2022/23 season, Southampton, Leicester and Leeds all fired their managers and all were relegated.

'This will be a horrible day for you. We at Everton feel very close to Manchester City – for a million and one reasons! You have an excellent set-up, an excellent board, an excellent manager and terrific supporters. We both need each other to be in the Premier League and, although I am sure that the feeling is one of emptiness today, I do sincerely believe, alongside all genuine football lovers in this country, that you will be back with us in 12 months' time. I salute the spirit in you.'

I got on very well with Everton, especially with their chairman, Philip Carter. When you went to Goodison Park, everything was very formal, lovely and old-fashioned. The Everton chairman would make a speech and you would respond. Their board was charming, win or lose.

Even after the loss at Portman Road, I was not wholly convinced Joe needed to go. On the Thursday evening, three days before the last game of the season, at home to Chelsea, I arranged to meet Joe at the Darbar, a restaurant on Rusholme's Curry Mile, which we had been to several times before. We did not need to order anything; the courses, as if by magic, simply appeared.

When I arrived, it was not a foregone conclusion we would decide to dismiss him. I took with me a list of

13 points I wanted Joe to respond to. Had he shown any recognition that they needed addressing, he might well have taken Manchester City into the new season. It was only when he rebuffed each of my arguments that I concluded there could be no way back.

When I got there, I asked Joe how he was feeling. 'Down but on the way up,' was the reply. When I asked him how he felt the season had gone, Joe replied that the players had not been adequate, the challenge of the Premier League had been underestimated and we had been very unlucky. He thought City needed to trim the squad by 10 to 12 players.

The first point I raised was Manchester City's scouting. We thought we relied far too much on scouts in the North West and the Midlands. For one game at Watford, my son, Richard, was asked if he fancied going to Vicarage Road to scout a player. Richard was very keen on football but would be the first to admit he was not a professional scout. Our overseas scouting was rudimentary. We had employed Jean-Luc Witzel, an agent, to be our French scout. In April 2001, which was the last board meeting Joe attended, we decided to investigate the expenses Witzel had submitted 'together with the related issues of matches attended and his employment status'.

We would not sign any players from France until Alioune Touré arrived from Nantes in September 2001 to join Kevin Keegan's side. The club used the Scottish agent, Willie McKay, who was based in Monaco and was setting himself up as a specialist in the French market. We were not alerted that the midfielder was on medication for blood clots and he developed deep vein thrombosis on a six-hour coach journey to Portsmouth. He played just one match for the club.

Joe conceded that Witzel was not good enough but denied this was an issue for himself or the chief scout, John Hurst. He had known and worked with Hurst for 35 years. They had played together at Everton and Hurst worked under Royle when he took over as manager at Goodison Park in 1994. He defended Hurst, as he defended all his staff. Nicky Weaver's performances in goal had declined significantly and there had been concerns about his drinking. When I mentioned Alex Stepney's performance as goalkeeping coach in this context, Royle responded that Stepney was 'very good'.

We had already agreed that Roy Bailey, the club's physiotherapist, should leave. Bailey had joined Manchester City as an apprentice in 1969 but a serious knee injury had cut short his playing career before it had properly begun. Joe Mercer had, however, given him a backroom job and he had become the club's physiotherapist. Peter Reid had fired him when he took over as manager in 1990, partly because Bailey allowed the comedian, Eddie Large, who was a passionate Manchester City fan, open access to the inner sanctums of the club, but Bailey had been brought back five years later.

However, Bailey did not have the qualifications the Premier League now required and we had taken the decision to replace him with Rob Harris, the physio for the Wigan Warriors rugby league team. Harris, who was from New Zealand, had just begun work at Carrington and Joe had agreed Roy would leave City at the end of the season. At the Darbar, Joe now said he had reconsidered and Roy should stay on. He said Harris had struggled to make an impression since his arrival and the staff would react badly because Bailey was a popular character. I was annoyed because this had already been agreed. Likewise, Joe acknowledged that there was little linkage between the academy and the first team but once more supported the man in position, the reserve-team manager, Asa Hartford, who had been a team-mate of Joe's at Manchester City.

It was the same with our desire to appoint a fitness coach. The outstanding candidate was a former Colombian midfielder, Juan Carlos Osorio, who had played and coached in the United States. He had a degree in exercise science from South Connecticut University and a diploma in science and football from Liverpool John Moores University. He had been working with the New York MetroStars (now New York Red Bulls) and had impressed me, Dennis Tueart and Willie Donachie when he was interviewed. Joe, however, had reacted badly and had phoned Dennis to complain. 'How dare you hire staff without consulting me,' was how Dennis recalled Joe's reaction. Dennis thought that Willie would have passed the information on to his manager.

In the restaurant, Joe complained that Dennis was a 'busy bollocks' and was interfering too much. He again vetoed Osorio's appointment, saying he did not want a foreign coach. The coaches Joe Royle had surrounded himself with – men like Stepney, Hurst, Hartford and Bailey – were all his contemporaries. He had objected to Harris and Osorio, who were both younger and foreign. When Peter Schmeichel came to Manchester City in 2002, he described Harris and Osorio as the best physio and fitness coach he had worked with. Osorio would go on to manage Mexico in the 2018 World Cup in Russia.

I then raised the issue of drinking. As well as the £1,000 bill from the Forest of Arden, there had been a big drinks bill at the hotel before the game at Ipswich, one we needed to win to have any chance of surviving in the Premier League. I said: 'I cannot understand how drinking [by players] could be dealt with if the management were also heavily indulging?'

Joe's solution was that the management team should be limited to claiming £100 for drinks at every away match. When I asked if this was the total to be spent or claimed, Joe replied 'claimed'. He reserved the right to spend as much on drink as he liked. I told him his reply did not seem like a meeting of minds.

The dinner came to a strange end. Much to my surprise, Joe mentioned what his salary would be now that Manchester City had been relegated to the First Division. In the Premier League, Joe had been on £750,000 a year. This would be reduced to £150,000 a year, which he thought was insufficient. Joe then mentioned Harry Redknapp's recent dismissal by West Ham, adding Redknapp had received a substantial pay-off – the settlement of his contract and pension contributions had cost West Ham £3m. It was an odd way to end. I told Joe that how West Ham settled contracts was a matter for them.

By now, we were the only diners remaining in the Darbar. There had been a certain tension as the discussion went on, but it was very civilised – perhaps too civilised, because Joe never saw what was coming. The remark about Redknapp was the only indication Joe thought his position might have been in danger. He recalled: 'As I parted company with the chairman late that Thursday night, I had no inkling of the fate that would befall me.'

When I left the restaurant, I reluctantly realised we had no option but to part company with our manager. Joe's response to relegation was to keep all his existing staff, make no changes – except to what could be claimed for alcohol – and put our demotion down to ill luck and the fact we had underestimated the level of the Premier League. When Manchester City had last been relegated from the Premier League in 1996, the club had made no appropriate adjustments, beginning a process that ended up with the club relegated again. In 1996, City had been relegated on goal difference on the last afternoon of the season. In 2001, we were eight points from safety with the worst home record in the division. We could not go on as before.

The next day, Friday, 18 May, I called an emergency board meeting at the Crowne Plaza hotel in Manchester. In a three-hour meeting, I told the board about the discussions I had had with Joe and the issues I had raised with him. We had spent £17m on transfers and relegation would cost an estimated £15m. In the words of the minutes of that meeting: 'The chairman had received absolutely no response with regard to the need for change or development. In fact, the manager had expressed satisfaction with the set-up and had gone back on the decision to release Roy Bailey at the end of the season.

'The chairman then asked the board as to their views as to the action necessary and it was unanimously agreed to terminate the manager's contract as from next Monday. The subject of compensation was discussed and it was agreed to comply with the terms of the manager's contract.'

There was no final flourish on the pitch. We were beaten 2-1 by Chelsea. The next day, I had arranged to meet Joe in my office at Maine Road. With me were John Wardle and Bryan Bodek. The moment Joe came into the room and saw Bryan, his face fell. The presence of the club's lawyer could mean only one thing. I said: 'Joe, things haven't worked out. We went through all this on Thursday night, you showed no willingness to deal with the issues I have raised and I'm afraid we are going to have to part company.' He stormed out and slammed the door. It was done in two minutes. Stepney, Bailey and Hurst also had their contracts terminated. It was very unpleasant but that is the essential cruelty of football.

I liked Joe very much and working with him had given me one of the highlights of my lifetime. However, it was something that had to be done and, to quote *Macbeth*: 'If it were done when 'tis done then 'twere well if it were done quickly.'

Joe had been an outstanding manager for Manchester City in the Football League. The challenges of the Premier League were different and changing rapidly. Dennis Tueart compared Joe to Sunderland's most famous manager, Bob Stokoe, who had beaten Don Revie's Leeds to win the FA Cup in 1973. However, when Sunderland were promoted to the top division three years later, Stokoe resigned after failing to win a single match. There is a statue of Stokoe outside Sunderland's Stadium of Light and, because of the play-off final and the two promotions, there would always be a place for Joe in Manchester City's heart.

Once the decision had sunk in, Joe recognised that, having relegated a club from the Premier League, any manager would have been fortunate to have survived. However, he objected fiercely to our offer that we would compensate him as a First Division rather than a Premier League manager. This was nonsense. We had been relegated and were now a First Division club. We were compensating him exactly in accordance with the terms of his contract. He was paid £150,000 less tax and national insurance.

When you are relegated, your share certificate in the Premier League has to be signed and transferred to one of the three promoted clubs – in our case one of Fulham, Blackburn and Bolton. This was not done until 28 May, after Bolton had beaten Preston in the play-off final. Joe's lawyers claimed that because Manchester City still held the Premier League share certificate when he was dismissed, he should be compensated as a Premier League manager. Joe was basing his case on a technicality, hiding behind legalese. Morally, he could not argue we were any longer a Premier League club.

There was a hearing at the High Court in Liverpool in July 2004, where I was called as a witness. Joe won his case and was awarded £423,000 in damages. The club overturned the decision in the Court of Appeal in London eight months later and Joe was ordered to repay the award and pay £80,000 costs. It was a case he should never have pursued.

Both Dennis and I fell out very badly with Joe and neither of us have spoken to him since. I am sad about it to this day. I met his son, Darren, at a football event some years later and I told him I would love to get together with his father once more but nothing ever came of it. Football can foster some very intense friendships but it says something for the pressures of the game that many of them break and, when they are broken, they are sometimes fractured beyond repair.

> **Chris Bird:** After David's meeting with Joe on the Curry Mile, I had a phone call from Willie Donachie, who wanted to meet me at the club. He said it was not working and City needed to move forward. Willie was a progressive. He was into the new training and nutrition regimes that Arsène Wenger had brought in at Arsenal. I think he had got to the point where he thought this was no longer Joe's game. I would always meet Joe after a home game for a drink. At the last match of the season, at home to Chelsea, I knew he was going. I went into the chairman's lounge and he asked me if I wanted

a drink. I made my excuses and said, 'Sorry, Joe, I've got something on,' and waved him goodbye. The next time he saw me, he went up to me and said: 'You bastard, you knew and you never told me.' I told him I couldn't tell him. I worked for the board. It wasn't my place.

The Keegan Effect

THERE WAS a reason we could not delay Joe Royle's dismissal; we knew Kevin Keegan was interested in the Manchester City job. We knew, too, that his enthusiasm had a habit of waning.

As with Joe, the initial contact had been made by Dennis Tueart. Although he had made his footballing name in Sunderland's FA Cup-winning team, Dennis had been born in Walker, in the East End of Newcastle, where the cranes of the Swan Hunter shipyard dominated the skyline. He had come to know Keegan when business took him to St James' Park shortly after Kevin had begun his remarkable transformation of Newcastle United. Keegan said he would only talk to Manchester City once there was a managerial vacancy. We had not yet dismissed Joe.

By the spring of 2001, Keegan's career was perhaps at its lowest ebb. Before becoming England manager, his time in football had been one of almost unbroken rolling success. As a player, he had won the league, the FA Cup and the European Cup with Liverpool. He had left to play for Hamburg, where he had won the Bundesliga and been voted European Footballer of the Year. In 1982, he had joined Newcastle, who were then in the Second Division. His final appearance at St James' Park had seen him helicoptered from the centre circle after Newcastle had regained top-flight status. He was one of the first celebrity footballers, made wealthy by advertising endorsements.

In 1992, he had returned to Tyneside to manage a Newcastle side seemingly resigned to relegation to the Third Division. Fourteen months later, he had promoted them to the Premier League with a thrilling brand of football. The epic struggle with Manchester United for the title in 1996 was credited with establishing the Premier League's hold on audiences and justifying Sky Sports' investment in it.

In the season before he returned to manage Newcastle, the average attendance at St James' Park was 16,800 – comparable with Southampton, Norwich and Oldham. In the summer of 1996, roughly that number would come to the stadium to see Alan Shearer sign a contract after Newcastle had broken the world transfer fee record to bring the England captain back to his home city. Keegan was intelligent and articulate. At Newcastle, he would sometimes give two press conferences a day – one for the evening papers and another for the morning editions. He spoke German and Spanish. The media adored him. He was box office.

However, in early January 1997, he resigned, a decision that led television news bulletins. Newcastle United were changing to become a public limited company. Keegan could no longer simply call the club chairman, Sir John Hall, and ask for more spending. It had to be justified to the plc board. Newcastle could not really afford Shearer and there had to be the kind of cutbacks that made Keegan uncomfortable. As the financial taps were turned off, Newcastle began sliding. He started disliking the press conferences, which became more infrequent. He told Newcastle's chief executive, Freddie Fletcher, he would resign at the end of the season. Then the board informed him it would be better for everyone if he left immediately.

After a brief, lucrative interlude at Fulham, where he worked for Mohamed Al Fayed in the third tier of English football, he succeeded Glenn Hoddle as England manager. However, the European Championship in Holland and Belgium had been a disaster and defeat by Germany at

Wembley imperilled qualification for the World Cup in Japan and South Korea. Keegan resigned, admitting he was tactically unsuited to international football management. That was October 2000. He had not worked since.

I had been warned off Keegan by one or two people who had got to know him. 'Make sure you know what you're doing,' they said. 'You might end up holding a tiger by the tail.' Chris Bird and I had been keen on David Moyes, who but for defeat in the play-off final would have promoted Preston from the third tier to the Premier League. However, Moyes had just turned 38, had never played or managed in the English top flight and had just signed a five-year contract at Deepdale.

Keegan was still box office and, despite his failures with England, the scale of his achievements on Tyneside could not be dismissed. Newcastle and Manchester City were similar clubs in size and in the passion of their fanbase. We needed an instant impact and Keegan was a man who made instant impacts. The cost of relegation was around £15m to Manchester City and John Wardle and David Makin, as the board members who had put most money into the club, were eager to appoint someone who delivered swift results.

Once Joe had left the club, Dennis called Kevin again and arranged a meeting at his home. Kevin was still living in the North East. Sir John Hall, who had by now stepped down as Newcastle chairman, had bought Wynyard Park, a Victorian mansion in County Durham, and Keegan rented one of the houses on the estate. Despite his falling-out with the board at St James' Park, he still enjoyed a good relationship with his landlord.

I was under considerable pressure to return with Keegan as our next manager. At a meeting before I went up to the North East, David Makin had come over to me and said: 'We've got to get him. Don't behave like an accountant.' I interpreted that advice as an instruction not to over-negotiate and ensure we brought Kevin back to Manchester. The meeting was pleasant, if brief. Keegan was clearly interested in coming to Manchester City and we got down to the finances pretty quickly. I offered him a salary of £500,000 and the same figure as a promotion bonus. He said: 'Chairman, I don't need any incentive to win promotion. Just give me a salary of £1m.' I might have negotiated harder but, given the result my shareholders expected me to deliver, my only response was: 'Yes, Kevin.' I might inadvertently have given Keegan the impression I was an easy touch.

We were very keen to keep Willie Donachie, who was a quiet, studious coach. I think he understood some of the issues I raised with Royle towards the end and he would certainly have embraced the training revolution Arsène Wenger had begun in Premier League football. However, Kevin wanted his own assistant, Arthur Cox, who had been his manager when he was a player at Newcastle. He had wanted Arthur as his assistant at England but the FA had vetoed the appointment because, at 59, they considered Cox too old. Donachie was offered the post of first-team coach but left to join Sheffield Wednesday.

When Kevin appeared at Maine Road for his press conference on Thursday, 24 May, there were crowds waiting for him. Not since Malcolm Allison had Manchester City possessed a manager with Keegan's kind of charisma. Our fans had lived in Manchester United's shadow for a decade and now we had appointed the one manager who seemed able to stand up to Sir Alex Ferguson. This was a sign that, despite relegation, Manchester City was a club that was still prepared to think big.

Speaking to journalists with his old fervour, the comparisons were all with Newcastle rather than England. 'We proved in two or three years at Newcastle what you can

City players protest as referee Graham Poll awards a penalty to Liverpool. February 2001.

Roy Keane stand over Alfie Haaland in the wake of the United captain's reckless, premeditated tackle at Old Trafford.

With City vice-chairman, John Wardle, and Prince Charles.

Beginning what would be a roller-coaster ride with Kevin Keegan, May 2001.

Ali Benarbia and Eyal Berkovic – an Algerian Muslim and an Israeli Jew – would become the fulcrum of our midfield.

Take a bow; Kevin Keegan delivered promotion with all the panache he promised.

Signing Nicolas Anelka was a huge statement of intent from a newly promoted club.

Anelka destroys United's defence in the final Manchester derby at Maine Road, November 2002.

Gary Neville mocked by City fans as City score again at Maine Road.

The King of the Kippax *reacts to my departure in March 2003.*

With Prince William and Kate at the National Football Centre during my time as FA chairman.

Playing golf with England manager, Roy Hodgson.

With Roy Hodgson on a pilgrimage to Auschwitz during Euro 2012 in Poland and Ukraine.

At Wembley with Sir Bobby Charlton.

Khaldoon Al Mubarak joins me at the 2013 FA Cup Final. Past and present chairmen were about to watch a 'typical City' performance against Wigan.

Meeting Queen Elizabeth at Windsor while chairman of the British Red Cross.

Receiving the CBE for services to football in 2014.

do. Once you get the momentum going and get everyone rowing the same way, you take it way beyond what the most optimistic person thinks,' he said. Kevin admitted he had neither discussed transfer budgets nor had he seen the training facilities at Carrington. He said he could foresee a time when Manchester City overtook Manchester United as a football force. City, he predicted, would be challenging for the title in five years. For the assembled press, the headlines wrote themselves.

There was something of Boris Johnson in watching Keegan's public appearances. He had a fantastic persona which would make people like him immediately, even if they were disposed not to. At the same time, I did not think there was a great deal of intellectual depth there – both went for broad brush strokes rather than fine detail. Both were great enthusiasts who were easily bored. Dennis thought Kevin's shelf-life as a manager was three years. He had signed a five-year contract.

The first thing I talked to Kevin about was the drinking culture at the club. He acted quickly and decisively, calling a team meeting to stress that football had changed. He sold Mark Kennedy to Wolverhampton Wanderers for £1.5m. He thought Kennedy was one of City's better players but he also wanted to break up what he called 'the gang of boozers' although, when it was put to me, I was told it would be for football reasons.

The club had just started pre-season training when Kevin decided to spend the day house-hunting in Hale, an affluent village where Greater Manchester meets the Cheshire countryside. He went into a restaurant called the Up and Down – which was an apt name for a Manchester City manager to choose. Once inside, he saw Steve Howey and Jeff Whitley sharing a bottle of champagne. Howey had played for Keegan at Newcastle but he turned 30 in October and age, allied to a questionable attitude to alcohol, meant he was not the force he had been at St James' Park. He was sold to Leicester in 2003. Whitley would be loaned out to Notts County and released in March 2002. He would become a full-blown alcoholic and cocaine user before kicking the habit. The catalyst was meeting an old friend at a hotel in Stockport in November 2007. Whitley caught sight of a ragged face in a mirror and did not recognise himself.

Keegan kept faith with Nicky Weaver in goal until he seriously injured his knee playing at Birmingham in March 2002, although Kevin informed us during the summer that he had been fined for drinking during his rehabilitation.

We would eventually send him to Richard Parker, the same specialist in Ohio who had treated Paulo Wanchope's knee injury. Weaver would not start a first-team match for Manchester City until August 2006. A year later, he moved to Charlton.

Kevin's most intractable problem was Richard Dunne's drinking. Dunne was a young Irish international defender whom Joe had bought from Everton for £3m. He still lived in Southport, would frequently be out in the pubs and clubs of Merseyside and was probably a stone overweight. In October 2001, Keegan, who did not always attend board meetings, told us that he had fined Dunne two weeks' wages for twice failing to report for training. He had also asked him to move to Manchester.

Eleven months later, when he turned up to Carrington late and looking dishevelled, Keegan not only fined Dunne but threatened to ask us to terminate his contract. This produced a startling reaction in Dunne, who left Southport, stopped drinking and began training at eight in the morning with the staff before joining the first-team squad. He would stay with Manchester City until 2009.

There were some players Keegan inherited from Joe that he was unable to transform. One was Laurent Charvet, a French full-back whom Joe had signed from Newcastle for £1m. Charvet had not been an outstanding performer at St James' Park and nor was he at Maine Road. Kevin considered him a liability and told the board he had asked Charvet to leave training because he was showing so little effort. He would play only three times for Keegan before returning to France with Sochaux, where he did not play at all.

Keegan thought that without Andy Morrison, whose Maine Road career was coming to an end because of his knee injuries, the club lacked a dressing-room leader. It was why he decided to bring in Stuart Pearce, who was now 39, as club captain. The two most impactful signings, however, were an Algerian and an Israeli. To sign Ali Benarbia and Eyal Berkovic, two midfielders who did not defend very much and were not overly keen to do any tackling, was a very brave move for a manager contemplating a season in the second tier of English football. It emphasised that Kevin saw Manchester City as a team that would attack the division. There are some managers who would have asked for one of those players, but not both. But he did it and it worked.

Keegan admitted he had never heard of Benarbia. He was 32 and was captain of Paris Saint-Germain. In September

2001, his agent, Willie Mackay, who had brokered what proved a very unsuccessful deal for Alioune Touré, was taking him from Manchester Airport to Sunderland for a trial when he phoned Keegan and asked to meet him for lunch at Carrington. While in the canteen, Arthur Cox pointed out that after Keegan had quit Newcastle, they had played a UEFA Cup quarter-final against Monaco and the footballer in the corner of the room had destroyed them in midfield.

When Benarbia and Mackay arrived on Wearside for the trial, the Sunderland manager, Peter Reid, failed to turn up. Kevin arranged a trial for him at Carrington and described Ali as 'an island of composure'. Paris Saint-Germain were prepared to let him go on a free transfer. He cost us £2,000 a week in wages and a £250,000 bonus when Manchester City were promoted. Money was relatively tight at City – Alistair Mackintosh had budgeted for a seventh-place finish – and Kevin got a signing he still regards as perhaps the best he ever made, certainly in terms of value for money. Benarbia was allowed to fly back to France to collect his belongings and put straight into the team to face Birmingham at Maine Road.

He said he was surprised a Second Division fixture should have attracted such a big crowd. When he went to take a corner after 20 minutes, his play had been so mesmeric that the crowd gave him a standing ovation. He would learn, as Colin Bell and Georgi Kinkladze learned, that Maine Road was a stadium that adored pure football skill. Birmingham were beaten 3-0. They would return the following month for a League Cup tie and would lose 6-0. Benarbia had an ability to find Shaun Goater that the striker likened to a satnav. Their partnership would open up the highway to promotion. The chants from the stands were all about 'Feeding the Goat'.

Kevin found Berkovic much harder to manage and in this he was not alone. At West Ham, there had been an infamous training ground fight with John Hartson while his manager, Harry Redknapp, was being interviewed on television a few yards away. Celtic had paid £5.75m for him but he had a habit of criticising his manager, Martin O'Neill, in print. O'Neill loaned him out to Blackburn. Kevin signed him for £1.5m. It showed football's ability to cross divides that an Israeli Jew and an Algerian Muslim should form one of Manchester City's most effective midfield partnerships.

Berkovic was, however, a dreadful trainer. I was doing a lot of running at the time and would have quite fancied my chances of beating him over a couple of laps of the Carrington training ground. Berkovic never stopped being opinionated. Kevin had given me a standing invitation to the dressing room to hear his pre-match talk. He said he wanted to demonstrate to his players that we were a team, from the dugout to the boardroom. It was a real privilege to watch him going about his business at such close quarters. His delivery varied a lot. Sometimes, his powers of motivation would seem extraordinary. Sometimes, he could be strangely negative or he would turn up late.

On one occasion, I had gone down to the dressing room and, despite the fact that we had won the previous week, Kevin seemed to be in a bad mood, ranting away very negatively. He was facing me but with his back to Eyal Berkovic. Just then, I caught Berkovic's eye. H1e pointed at his manager and mouthed the word 'meshuga', which is Yiddish for 'crazy'.

You were never quite sure which Kevin Keegan you were going to get. Perhaps that was no bad thing. It would keep his message fresh and his players interested. I am sure that football management is not primarily about tactics, it is about motivating a disparate group of people over a long period of time. It is why the great managers, people like

Brian Clough, Sir Alex Ferguson and Arsène Wenger were, at their core, highly intelligent people with a great insight into the psyche of their players. As a manager, Kevin was more of a sprinter than a marathon runner. He achieved great initial impacts but was unable to sustain them, which may explain why, after nearly five years at first Newcastle and then Manchester City he felt he had become stale, had lost the ability to motivate and he resigned.

At the start, he moved quickly. A little over a month after his appointment, Dennis told the board that Cox had reorganised the club's scouting system, while Juan Carlos Osorio had signed a three-year contract with City. With more than a month to go until our opening fixture against Watford, we had sold 22,851 season tickets, which had brought in £6.7m. Paulo Wanchope was removed from the transfer list.

We made a dramatic start. Watford, now managed by Gianluca Vialli, were beaten 3-0 at Maine Road. The next three home games, against Crewe, Birmingham and Walsall, were won by a collective scoreline of 11-2. When Wimbledon beat us 4-0 on 29 September, it would be the only game Manchester City would lose at home all season. Away from Maine Road, City's form was more mixed. Until

1 December, we had won only three times – although one of those was a 6-2 demolition of Sheffield Wednesday at Hillsborough.

We went to Grimsby sitting in eighth place. City won 2-0 at Blundell Park. The next fixture would also be away, at Millwall on a Tuesday night.

We had an issue with Millwall that ran back to February 1999 when we were both in Division Two. Groups of hooligans had come up from London to have pre-arranged fights with their City counterparts. There was trouble inside the ground and violence that drew police dressed in riot gear into the streets outside Maine Road. As I was travelling back down to London in heavy rain, I took a call from the club's head of security saying that City fans were attacking the Millwall team bus and asking what he should do. I told him he should take responsibility and do his job – one he would lose the following day. To have to call me in the middle of the motorway to seek advice on doing something that seemed perfectly obvious was absurd.

City had not played Millwall since but the animosity between the two sets of fans was so intense that the Football League had banned both fixtures from having away supporters. It was decided that, aside from the team and

Kevin's backroom staff, I would be Manchester City's only official representative at the New Den. I met the team in a hotel in south London and got on the coach with them. We had an unusually heavy police escort.

The atmosphere was unremittingly hostile with one end of the ground completely empty. Kevin was sent off and made his way to the directors' box. As he sat down next to me, a group of Millwall fans turned to us and made throat-slitting gestures. Shaun Goater recalled that, even by Millwall's notorious standards, the racism directed at himself and Shaun Wright-Phillips was as bad as he had ever known. He thought the club should be shut down. Benarbia was howled down because he was Muslim, Berkovic because he was Jewish. Fittingly, Wright-Phillips scored the winner, a beautiful, curling shot from distance, seven minutes from time. It was his first goal for the club. When some City fans, who had hired an executive box to beat the ban, celebrated, the box was besieged by Millwall supporters from the Family Enclosure.

Keegan thought the 3-2 victory was the turning point in the season. Some of the football produced was as good as any I had seen a City side produce. We won 15 successive matches at Maine Road. We put five past Burnley and

Barnsley and four past Grimsby, Gillingham, Sheffield Wednesday and Coventry. Perhaps of more significance was overcoming Wolves, Norwich, Nottingham Forest and Crystal Palace while only conceding once.

Kevin would, in the following seasons, become very critical of what he saw as our failure to back him financially. However, at a board meeting on 20 December 2001, a few days after a 3-1 win over Bradford had sent City to second in Division One, it was noted: 'The board unanimously agreed that the manager should be given every support and, if possible, additional resources should be made available to strengthen our promotion push. It was therefore agreed to approach our bankers for £5m of additional funding.'

We won the First Division championship with 99 points, having scored 108 goals – equalling a club record. In 1926/27 Manchester City had also scored 108 times, which had not been enough to secure promotion to Division One.

That season, City had finished third behind runaway champions Middlesbrough and second-placed Portsmouth, who had scored 21 fewer but had the same number of points and the protection of a better goal average. This time, there was clear sky-blue water between us and everyone else. We were ten points clear of West Brom in second. They had scored 47 fewer goals.

The comparisons were always with Keegan's achievements at Newcastle. Poignantly, Manchester City were drawn to play them at St James' Park in the FA Cup. There were crowds of Newcastle fans to welcome Kevin 'home' and a reminder that his relationship with the Newcastle manager, Bobby Robson, had not always been easy. Robson had ended Keegan's England playing career and was irritated by claims Keegan had made Newcastle a 'big club'. He pointed out that Newcastle 'had been a big club in 1951 when I queued for an FA Cup Final ticket and couldn't get one'. The match itself was an anticlimax. Richard Dunne was sent off after 29 minutes and Newcastle won 1-0. On leaving St James' Park, I saw Bobby walking towards Newcastle Station to get the train home, which seemed like a scene from another age. We were able to give him a lift.

Keegan had delivered promotion with all the panache he had promised and it did bear comparisons with Newcastle. In 1993, they had won promotion to the Premier League with 96 points and 92 goals. City had bettered those statistics. That season on Tyneside had been the start of something spectacular. There were many who had the same hopes for Manchester City.

When Newcastle had been promoted, Keegan had written a piece in the programme under the headline: 'Alex, We're Coming for Your Title'. This time, he did not make predictions anything like as bold – not least because Arsenal, rather than Manchester United, had won the Premier League – although that did not stop others. A friend, Cambridge historian and passionate Manchester City fan Colin Shindler, had published a best-selling account of his love affair with Maine Road, called *Manchester United Ruined My Life*. Now, in the *Daily Mail*, beneath a photograph of Keegan parading the championship trophy around the stadium, he compared this team to the one that had won promotion to the old First Division in 1966.

'That City team was far from the finished article. Yet, we had "Sha-la-la-la" Summerbee marauding down the right, Mike Doyle improving with every match at right-half and Colin Bell, our £45,000 record signing from Bury. And, like the team of Joe Mercer and Malcolm Allison, who went on to become league champions in 1968, Kevin Keegan's Manchester City can only get better … Thank you, Kevin, for a season none of us will ever forget.

'Now, all we ask is the Premier League title in two years' time.'

There was genuine excitement among supporters that Maine Road's final season would, like its first, be in English football's top flight. We were offering a two-year season ticket which covered the farewell season at Maine Road and the first at the City of Manchester Stadium. By March 2002, with promotion still not quite confirmed, 85 per cent of City season ticket holders indicated they would be taking the two-year deals. By July, we had sold 18,800 season tickets for a 2003/04 season for which we could not guarantee which division we would be playing in. Those fans had, in effect, loaned their club £3m. Seventeen months before the new stadium opened, all but eight executive boxes had been sold. Joe Royle had confessed we had underestimated the competitiveness of the Premier League when Manchester City were last promoted. John Wardle and David Makin agreed to loan the club £6.15m for player recruitment.

I enjoyed being the public face of the club, especially at times like these. Public speaking was one of the tasks of a chairman and, in May 2002, Leeds had made headlines when inviting the comedian Stan Boardman to speak at a tribute dinner for Rio Ferdinand. Boardman had made a

I should have got one or two more goals but, with all the talk about becoming the first City player since Francis Lee to score 30 in a season, I started to tense up. With just a few matches remaining, I told myself, 'Just relax and go out and play,' and the 30th goal arrived (in a 3-1 win at Crewe in March). That season, I was playing up front with Darren Huckerby, who liked to go out wide. He would get the ball, draw out defenders and leave loads of space for me in the middle. Darren scored 26 goals that season.

Chris Bird: I had been given the task of finding a new training ground. Dennis Tueart and I knew a property developer, Andy Shaw, who was European director for Jones Lang Lasalle, a massive American real estate company. I rang and asked if he could help us. Andy rang back and said: 'I think I might have found you the place. It's owned by Manchester University and it's in Carrington. They want half a million quid for it.' It was exactly what we needed. It would have a media room, a proper medical centre, a gym, a pool and it had privacy, which is something Platt Lane never possessed. Nicolas Anelka told me that Carrington was better than Real Madrid's training ground and in 2002, when he came to us, Real Madrid were European champions.

We laid new pitches at Carrington and it was touch and go as to whether they would be ready to train on at the start of the season. Keegan said: 'Can you guarantee me that the pitches will be ready when the players get back for pre-season?' I replied: 'As best I can, yes.' In the first board meeting after the players returned, Keegan complained that the pitches weren't right, that they were too hard.

He turned to me and said: 'You deceived me.' I replied: 'Who the hell do you think you are?' We almost had to be separated. Keegan did not speak to me for six weeks. In that time, I had to sit with him at every press conference, travel on the team bus with him and see him after matches. In that time, there was nothing from him but silence. Then one Saturday morning, David Makin told me it was his little lad's birthday and could we arrange a five-a-side at the training ground. Shortly after we arrived at Carrington, Kevin Keegan pulled in. He said: 'I hear you've got a five-a-side on; I've come to help.'

He asked if I fancied a cup of tea and, when we were standing in the kitchen looking out of the window, he said: 'Just so you know, I was out of order.' From that moment on, we had a great relationship.

The Lifeboat

WEDNESDAY, 2 September 1998, was not an obvious landmark in the history of Manchester City. Even Shaun Goater might struggle to recall his two goals against Walsall that pushed City into eighth place in League Division Two. It was, however, a day that would change Manchester City forever. It was the day the agreement was signed to build a stadium in Manchester for the Commonwealth Games, a stadium that would become our home. Fifteen months later, the prime minister, Tony Blair, would lay the foundation stone. In August 2003, Manchester City took possession of this fabulous venue.

It is hard to imagine what would have happened to Manchester City had we stayed at Maine Road. Most probably, we would have become an Everton, a club with a great history, deep support and, until their move to a new venue on the Mersey, an ageing, atmospheric stadium but not one of the main players in European or even Premier League football. The investors from Abu Dhabi would never have been interested in taking over Maine Road. They had, briefly, examined Everton as a target but concluded that Goodison Park was beyond redevelopment. St James' Park needed very little work but the Newcastle owner, Mike Ashley, would not sell. Not only were Manchester City keen to sell, but they also possessed a new stadium.

The City of Manchester Stadium – I can claim credit for suggesting the name – would occupy an increasing part of my time and that of Alistair Mackintosh. The stock photograph of me in the *Manchester Evening News* saw me in a hard hat and high-visibility jacket surrounded by cranes as the stadium took shape.

The site of the stadium was in Eastlands, one of the most industrialised parts of Manchester, centred on Bradford Colliery, which closed in 1968. There was still plenty of high-grade coal to mine but, because the pit was so close to the city centre, it would be too disruptive and expensive to extend the workings. It meant there was a largely derelict, brownfield site near the middle of Manchester, awaiting an opportunity to be developed.

The city council thought the moment had come in 1993 when Manchester launched its bid for the 2000 Olympics with plans for an 80,000-capacity stadium on the Eastlands site. The Games, however, were awarded to Sydney. The focus shifted to the 2002 Commonwealth Games. London had also bid to stage the Games but lost the vote 17-7 to Manchester.

The original proposals had been scaled down and the Commonwealth stadium, which would stage the athletics and the opening and closing ceremonies, would now be a 48,000-capacity venue. Its eventual cost of £110m would be funded mainly by Sport England with 30 per cent coming from Manchester City Council. The question then arose of what the legacy would be.

There were suggestions, articulated by people like Seb Coe, that once the Games were over the City of Manchester Stadium should become a centre of British athletics and should bid to stage the 2005 World Athletics Championships. However, there was not sufficient demand to fill a 48,000-seat stadium each summer and, in any case, London was planning its own athletics stadium, at Pickett's Lock in Enfield, to host the championships. Unlike the City of Manchester Stadium, Pickett's Lock became a developmental fiasco and the championships had to be shifted to Helsinki.

Football was the only sport that could regularly fill a major stadium. Manchester United had not the slightest interest in leaving Old Trafford. The only possible candidate was Manchester City – and that was to give us considerable leverage when it came to negotiating with the city council. This contrasted with the London Olympic Stadium. Tottenham, West Ham and Leyton Orient all expressed their interest in moving in once the 2012 Games were done. There was also an insistence that it should be maintained as an athletics venue.

This was not the case in Manchester and some, like the former Newcastle chairman, Sir John Hall, would express their astonishment at what a good deal City were given, with the implication that there must have been some dodgy dealing along the way. Nothing could be further from the truth. The chief reason Manchester City got such a bargain was that we were the only game in town.

Negotiations between the club and the council began when Francis Lee was chairman, although I would almost always represent Manchester City. Once I became chairman, I would lead the negotiations alongside Alistair

Mackintosh. In May 1997, I wrote to the council's chief executive, Howard Bernstein – no relation, though he was a City fan – setting out the terms under which we would be prepared to move.

The negotiations with the various institutions involved were lengthy, detailed and technical, but carried out in a positive atmosphere with a real feel of co-operation. Ours was a very small team which, at the same time, was running every other aspect of the club. We realised that, although we were providing a minor part of the financing, our negotiating position was strong. We were the only serious potential occupants for such a large stadium and the city council and Sport England wanted a prestigious, permanent stadium and not a temporary structure. Great credit must be paid to Alistair, who performed strongly to bring this to such a positive conclusion.

There had yet to be a spade in the ground at Eastlands or even a contract to say the stadium would be built, but the assumption was that we would be ready to move in time for the 2000/01 season. Given that the Commonwealth Games were scheduled to run between 25 July and 4 August 2002, we would have to make some serious adjustments once we had taken possession of what would still be a building site.

I told Howard there was no possibility of City agreeing to move into a half-completed stadium and play there while it was finished off. I wrote: 'Once Manchester City move into the stadium, under no circumstances can the club vacate the stadium for a year to allow it to be completed. We must have permanent occupation after we leave Maine Road.

'We need to move into a stadium that is substantially complete as we cannot expect our supporters to watch or our team to play in a ground that is half-built and lacks the necessary atmosphere.' The obvious conclusion was that Manchester City would move in after the Games.

In those early days of discussions, the stadium's capacity was set at around 60,000. I suggested it should be nearer 70,000. I wrote: 'This capacity might enable lower prices to be charged, thereby maximising the chances of filling the stadium for major non-MCFC events. A smaller capacity (say 50,000) could enhance the perception that the stadium is being built for MCFC as opposed to being "The Stadium of the North".'

Then, there had been suggestions that Manchester should become the home of the new 'National Stadium' when the old Wembley was demolished in 2000. Unlike Birmingham, which became the main challenger to a redeveloped Wembley, Manchester would already have a stadium. However, this was a race Wembley would easily win.

When Queen Elizabeth visited Manchester, she was fascinated by a model of the stadium that swung round, showing how it would be transformed from an athletics to a football venue. The day after the closing ceremony, watched by Her Majesty in driving Manchester rain, work began to turn it into a 48,000-capacity venue by digging down to reveal the 7,000 seats in the bottom tier that had been built below track level. The stadium was beautifully designed with a sweeping roof, masts topped with lights that rose 230ft high and spiral walkways that echoed the San Siro in Milan. As you approach Piccadilly Station on trains from Euston at night, the lights from the stadium masts are one of the most notable landmarks of the proud city of Manchester.

For a major British infrastructure project, the building of the City of Manchester Stadium went remarkably smoothly. Everything was delivered on time and pretty much on budget. The original allowance was £90m. It came in at £110m. The Commonwealth Games themselves were a huge success. The Velodrome would become the headquarters of British Cycling while the Manchester Aquatics Centre that hosted the swimming and diving would become an elite facility open to the public.

From the beginning, I laid out principles that the club stuck to. We had spent £16m on redeveloping the Kippax and we possessed a stadium that held 34,000. We could, if we needed to, stay at Maine Road. We agreed to pay the council a rent but only on income generated by crowds of more than 34,000. If we got 41,000 through the gate, we would pay the council a part of the income generated by the extra 7,000. The number of hospitality boxes and the potential to use the stadium as a music venue were far greater than anything we could have had at Maine Road.

It was a phenomenally good deal. It was one which, for political reasons, Manchester City Council could not allow to fail. Failure had been too recent an experience at Manchester City. It says something for the tightness of our finances at the time that we negotiated an agreement that, if we were not in the Premier League, we would be allowed to keep all the car-parking income.

The council and Sport England would pay the capital costs of the stadium and we would pay for its fitting-out to become a football ground. One thing we were adamant about was that the pitch would not have a running track around it once we took it over. We thought a track would allow the atmosphere inside the stadium to evaporate. When West Ham first moved into the London Olympic Stadium, the track was blamed for a marked lack of atmosphere compared to the bear pit that had been Upton Park.

Manchester is a city where colours matter. When the stadium was fitted out for the Commonwealth Games, it was important that the primary colour should be blue. We did not want our supporters sitting on red seats. When City moved in, our fans nicknamed it 'The Blue Camp' in a self-deprecating nod to the great arena in Barcelona. They could not imagine and nor could I that one day Manchester City's achievements would match and for a time eclipse those at the Nou Camp.

The official name of the ground was important. In the early documents, it is referred to as 'The Manchester Stadium' or 'The Commonwealth Stadium'. I suggested it should be called 'The City of Manchester Stadium'. The naming rights would be owned by the council and, after the rights were acquired by Etihad Airways in 2011, the council would be making £4m a year from the stadium. By that time, the vision of transforming Eastlands into 'Sport City' had been largely fulfilled.

Given how rooted football fans are in tradition and how much Maine Road was part of so many lives, there was surprisingly little opposition to leaving. Most supporters recognised this was a deal that had to be done. We did not, initially, think that Maine Road would have to be demolished. We thought it could be used by a rugby league side or by the region's major rugby union club, Sale Sharks.

Because Sale Sharks' chief executive Niels de Vos had also been on the Commonwealth Games organising committee, there was considerable interest in the deal, which was first proposed in December 2000. However, although Sale were desperate to move out of their cramped surroundings, Maine Road would have been simply too big an upgrade from their ground at Heywood Road, which had a capacity of 3,300. It would also need substantial renovation. In March 2003 Sale achieved a compromise by leasing Stockport's ground, Edgeley Park. The city council then announced that Maine Road would be demolished to make way for housing.

That our old home would be turned into accommodation meant something would be given back to the community in Moss Side. The stands of Maine Road had been something of a beacon for a very deprived area. Manchester City had done an immense amount of work with schools and community groups in Moss Side and, with our departure, that was lost.

One thing we did fear losing was the atmosphere because when Maine Road stirred itself it was an awesome sound. I don't think the City of Manchester Stadium was ever quite as intimidating, especially in our early seasons there. Whether it was because of the changing nature of a football audience with more middle-class fans removing the old sharp edges or because new stadia tend to dampen down noise, I cannot say. What I can say without equivocation is that the new stadium would stage bigger matches and provide the backcloth to probably the greatest rebirth the English game has seen.

> **Alistair Mackintosh:** David had a very good relationship with the city council, especially with its chief executive, Sir Howard Bernstein, which smoothed things through but, smooth as it turned out to be, the stadium took over my life. Everyone working on it knew it would be transformational for Manchester City. We had a deadline of the Commonwealth Games, which absolutely could not be moved and, as

that deadline loomed, every weekend was taken up by it. There were two stadiums, the temporary one for the Games and the permanent one which would become our home. The permanent one had to be ready before the temporary one and then the bottom tiers of the stands would be filled in to build the athletics track. Then, after the Games, the track would be dug up to expose the bottom tiers. We had to be ready first. We had to determine when we would start paying rent and what our share of the car park would be. For a 28-year-old accountant, this was beautiful work. We had to raise funds for the stadium to be kitted out how we wanted it, which meant executive boxes in the North Stand and lounges to generate income. But it went as well as any project I have been involved with, even to the extent that we wanted Barcelona to open the stadium and we got them.

We all knew that this was a chance to transform the club forever and if we had to give up nine months of our lives to make it happen, we had to do it. We arranged a long-term securitisation loan for £43m with two banks, AXA PPP and Banco Espirito Santo, that funded our development of the stadium at a low rate of interest. Everyone was aware of the financial crisis that was happening at Leeds and I was very aware that the window for this kind of loan was closing.

Chris Bird: There were hardly any City fans against the move from Maine Road. At the time, I wasn't surprised by this; afterwards, I was. At the time, the fans were completely understanding of what we wanted to do. There was an absolute trust in what today would be called 'the project'. We travelled to every supporters' club with players and directors and a model and plans of the stadium and we could show them where their seat would be. The supporters felt involved, they could pick their seats. We lost something with the move because we lost the ferocity of the old North Stand. The City of Manchester Stadium was simply not intimidating in the way Maine Road could be. But we had to change in other ways. At Maine Road, you couldn't get a decent bite to eat. Moss Side was in desperate need of regeneration. It could also be an uncomfortable place to be after a night match.

Dave Wallace: One long-serving City supporter said to me just before we left Maine Road: 'This has not been a happy place for a long time now.' Maine Road had gone from being able to hold 84,000 to a 35,000-seater stadium with a couple of temporary stands. It was time to move. I went on the radio with David Bernstein to discuss the move and he ended up saying: 'It's a first when a fanzine editor and a football club chairman agree with each other.' The transformation of what was a derelict part of Manchester is extraordinary. David did a crafty thing; he got all the fanzines and supporters' associations together, laid on a buffet and asked us what we thought of paying for a season ticket that covered the last season at Maine Road and the first season at the new stadium. Everyone backed him. Sheikh Mansour would never have come in if we were still in Maine Road.

'Chairman, Are You Sitting Down?'

ONE OF Kevin Keegan's phrases I liked to repeat in speeches and one he used on the phone when he wanted to broach the subject of an expensive signing that he thought would excite the fans was: 'Chairman, are you sitting down?'

There would have been many chairmen who would have wanted a stiff drink as well as an armchair if their manager had informed them he wanted to sign Nicolas Anelka. However, I greeted the idea with enthusiasm. Anelka was then still only 24 but, despite making an electric impact when signed by Arsène Wenger as a teenager, he had already gone through four enormous clubs – Paris Saint-Germain, Arsenal, Real Madrid and Liverpool. At Madrid, he had fallen out with his manager, Vicente del Bosque, and refused to train, telling the press: 'They treat me like a dog. I am alone against everyone.' He was then not yet 21.

He had returned to his first club, Paris Saint-Germain, but in January 2002 he was loaned to Liverpool for six months. Halfway through that loan period, the Liverpool manager, Gérard Houllier, was summoned to a meeting in Paris by Anelka's brothers, Claude and Didier, who were acting as his agents. When he learnt they had persuaded PSG to offer Nicolas for sale for a fee of €13m to any club that would pay it, Houllier lost his temper. He thought that, since Liverpool had resurrected his career, they should have been given first refusal or preferential treatment. He was astonished to hear from Wenger that Arsenal had already been asked if they wanted Anelka back.

Liverpool refused to pay the fee the Anelkas and, through them, PSG were demanding. They thought €13m was too much for a player of Anelka's dubious temperament and that the level of his wages would cause dissent in the dressing room. When back on Merseyside, Nicolas Anelka informed Houllier he was prepared to lower his salary to stay at Anfield; Houllier told him it was finished. He had already decided to buy the Senegal striker, El-Hadji Diouf, from Lens for £10m. He would prove to be one of Houllier's worst investments.

Kevin was prepared to take the risk with Anelka. He thought for pace only Thierry Henry matched him as a centre-forward and that he could deal with Claude and Didier. I also thought it a risk worth taking and was excited by the prospect. Anelka seemed precisely the kind of high-profile signing Manchester City should be interested in. However, if the price had been too much for Liverpool, who had finished second behind Arsenal in the Premier League, how would it make sense for a newly promoted club? The fee we were quoted was £13.6m – nearly three times the club-record £5m we had paid for Preston's Jon Macken in February – and we had a problem with cashflow. It seemed beyond our resources.

I prided myself on being a creative negotiator and by now I had become used to how football clubs were prepared to do business. What quickly became clear was that PSG, who had paid Real Madrid £22m to bring Anelka back to France, were chiefly interested in a big headline figure. They were not overly concerned with how that money was paid. Conversely, our main problem was cashflow. The negotiations were done over the phone and by email and eventually PSG accepted that the £13.6m could be paid in instalments over seven years. The Anelka brothers made £800,000 from Nicolas's transfer. We made £3.6m by selling Alioune Touré back to PSG.

When it came to selling Manchester City to Nicolas Anelka, it helped that Kevin Keegan was our manager because his name carried weight in Europe. The deal was done on 24 May, the anniversary of Kevin's appointment. In those 12 months, we had hired one of the most charismatic names in English football as our manager, been promoted as champions and now we had delivered a world-class centre-forward.

Kevin did not find Anelka easy to manage. He was aloof, he barely spoke to some of his team-mates – especially Eyal Berkovic – and there were some matches in which Anelka appeared uninterested. There were others in which he dazzled and his scoring ratio of 37 goals in 89 league games was better than at any club he played for in his career, including his brilliant beginning at Highbury.

We had also recruited a world-class goalkeeper. Peter Schmeichel may have been 38 but it had only been three years since he won the Treble with Manchester United. He had left Old Trafford in 1999 to play for Sporting Lisbon and then Aston Villa. There, he had enjoyed working under John Gregory but, when the manager was replaced by Graham Taylor, relationships had begun to sour. He came on a free transfer.

Like Anelka, Schmeichel was attracted by Keegan's name. However, as a manager he did not think Keegan in the same class as Sir Alex Ferguson and considered that he relied on the taciturn Arthur Cox as 'a comfort blanket'. In his autobiography, Schmeichel summed Kevin up: 'It was a decent squad and Keegan knew how to be competitive in the Premier League. He did what he had done throughout his career, which was to buy experienced players who could do the job and not worry too much about development.'

Schmeichel was injured when he came to City and since Nicky Weaver's knee injury required long-term rehabilitation and Carlo Nash, whom Joe Royle had signed from Stockport in 2001, was suffering from a minor injury, Keegan asked if we could take Tim Flowers on a three-month loan from Leicester. Nash recovered in time for our return to the Premier League, a 3-0 defeat at Leeds, and Schmeichel was available for the opening match at Maine Road, a 1-0 win over Newcastle.

There were plenty of other signings. Sylvain Distin came to bolster our central defence from PSG for £3.8m. Matias Vuoso, an Argentinian striker who had partnered Diego Forlan at Independiente, was bought for £3.5m. In January, Manchester United had paid £6.9m for Forlan, who proved a disappointment at Old Trafford. Forlan did at least play 98 times for United. Vuoso did not play at all for City and, after a single season, was loaned out to the Mexican side, Santos Laguna. Dennis Tueart would tell the board that, because of the money being spent on transfers, some players would have to be sold.

Our bankers, the Co-op, were also becoming jittery and not just because of the spending at Maine Road. As they outlined in a letter in July, they recognised the football landscape was changing and becoming more unstable. The Bosman Ruling, which allowed footballers to go on a free transfer at the end of their contract, was now seven years old and had been driving up wages from clubs frightened their key assets could leave for nothing.

As the bank pointed out, the consequences of relegation had been made more alarming by the collapse of ITV Digital. In June 2000, while Sky paid £1.1bn to cover the Premier League until 2004, the newly formed ITV Digital, backed principally by Carlton and Granada, tried to challenge Rupert Murdoch head-on by paying £315m to screen Football League and League Cup games.

It was the largest television deal offered to clubs who were not in the top flight. At Norwich, their majority shareholder, Delia Smith, estimated it would bring an extra £2m a year into Carrow Road. Across Division One, it led to an upswing in short-term spending, mainly on players. The television revenues were factored into cashflow projections.

The channel was a disaster. The set-top boxes and the signal were unreliable and the viewing figures pitiful. In September 2001, an attractive-looking fixture between Nottingham Forest and Bradford, two clubs that had until fairly recently been part of the Premier League, attracted an audience of around 1,000. Having worked out that the total cost to ITV Digital of screening the match was £1.2m, *The Guardian* gleefully reported that it would have been cheaper for the channel to have taken its viewers to the City Ground, put them all up in a five-star hotel and given them each £500 spending money.

On 27 March 2002, ITV Digital went into administration, still owing the Football League £180m. Fortunately, Manchester City were about to be promoted back into the Premier League, but for clubs like Coventry, who had gone down with us but failed to bounce back, the results were a series of player sales. Burnley were forced to sell their ground, Turf Moor, to their bankers. It showed just how important it was for City to have regained Premier League status at the first time of asking.

City have not been relegated since but, as we prepared for another top-flight campaign in the summer of 2002, it was a risk the bank had to consider. Manchester City had not survived in the Premier League since 1995. There had been two failed campaigns since and there was no guarantee there would not be a third. As that 2002/03 season unfolded, the consequences of the reckless overspending at Leeds United were becoming ever more apparent. Banks that were lending money across football wanted reassurances that what was happening at Elland Road could not happen elsewhere.

The board minutes of 19 September recorded: 'Discussions with the bank have been extremely difficult and the bank had been unsupportive and erratic in their dialogue with the club. The chairman reviewed events over the last four months and there were a number of occasions on which the bank had fallen short of appropriate support. Presently, the bank was offering a £5m [overdraft] facility and possibly a £2m seasonal increase but were asking for substantial security driven by a concern about the worst-case scenario.'

Because it would be our last at Maine Road, the 2002/03 season would always carry plenty of emotion. That summer, Manchester had hosted the Commonwealth Games in the stadium that, once the closing ceremony had ended, would be fitted out to become our football home.

For the last time, we took on Manchester United at Maine Road. The result was everything we could have dreamed of. Anelka outpaced Rio Ferdinand to put Shaun Goater through and, when Shaun's shot was saved by Fabien Barthez, Anelka buried the rebound. After Ole Gunnar Solskjaer had equalised past Schmeichel, Shaun dispossessed Gary Neville, who was trying to play the ball back to his keeper, and scored against the club that had released him as a teenager. When Goater scored his second of the match and our third, it was his 100th goal for Manchester City.

Not since September 1989, when City had destroyed United 5-1, had we won the Manchester derby. Then, Alex Ferguson had driven home to Wilmslow and gone straight to bed with a pillow over his head. Had Michael Knighton completed his takeover at Old Trafford, he would probably have been sacked. Now, he rounded on Ruud van Nistelrooy, who had been wonderfully shackled by his fellow Dutchman, Gerard Wiekens. Van Nistelrooy had swapped shirts and

Ferguson told his striker that, if he ever repeated the gesture, he would never play for Manchester United again.

He told the media that he should open the dressing-room doors so United's fans could let their players know how poor their performance had been. Despite the thrilling closeness of their rivalry when Kevin was at Newcastle, it was only the second time he had beaten Ferguson in the Premier League. Ferguson had the grace to go for a drink with our manager.

Although it did not happen very often, Ferguson knew how to deal with defeat. The media remember him as being better and more revealing when Manchester United had lost than when they had won. He fronted up. Kevin tended to disappear and, when he did give interviews after a loss, he would often deflect the blame, mainly towards his board of directors.

At Maine Road, there was the chairman's room, which we used for entertaining on matchdays. It was a small, intimate space, too small to serve food in but well supplied with Scotch whiskies. I loved going there after a midweek match, especially if City had won. Dennis Tueart would usually be there, as would one or two other former City footballers. We entertained many managers, including

George Graham and Alex Ferguson, and, after he had done his media duties, Joe Royle would come up for a drink and a chat. Noel Gallagher came up after a Saturday match, completely euphoric that we had won. He knelt down and kissed my shoes.

After one match, against Norwich, Delia Smith came to the chairman's room accompanied by a young boy wearing a Norwich kit. She was told that football kits were not allowed in the room and was refused entry. I don't know whether the boy was Delia's grandson but it may not have been coincidental that the next time we went to Carrow Road, which was understandably famed for its food, the Manchester City delegation was put on a distant table and served little better than cheese and crackers. I am pleased to say that relationships with football's queen of catering were swiftly restored.

Keegan, however, almost never went to the chairman's room. I remember going to Arsenal and seeing Arsène Wenger chatting to the directors and sponsors before a game. He saw it as part of his managerial duties and it gave the impression that there was a unity between the playing side and the rest of the club. However, behind the smile and the enthusiasm, Kevin was something of a loner. Glenn Hoddle, his predecessor as England manager, was now at Tottenham, where he gave the impression that dealing with directors and sponsors was not in his remit. Kevin was the same.

He had been a great footballer but he was not a typical football man. He was not one for reunion dinners and, when not managing, he seldom watched matches on television. His friends tended to be people away from the game. When he was at Liverpool, where there was a community of players in Southport and Formby, he had lived in the north Wales countryside. After retiring as a player in 1984, he had stepped away from football entirely, living in Marbella for eight years, playing golf and raising his family.

Keegan recalled in his autobiography that, when dealing with me, he did not like the word 'consolidation'. His regime would be about constant revolution, fed by a churn of players. There would be regular phone calls. At this time, I was chairman of a company based in Nuneaton. I was in the Midlands after a board meeting there when, waiting on a railway platform, my phone rang. 'Chairman, we need a quick decision. Arthur Cox has been offered double his salary to move and I can't afford to lose him. You've just got to pay him the money, David.'

There would be similar conversations about player salaries or signings. They were designed to put me in a corner. I don't think Kevin ever lied to me; there would always be some truth at the core of the conversation but he would frequently exaggerate for effect. If I said 'No' or 'Give me some time to think about it,' there would be a reaction. His voice would be raised, there would be complaints that I was ruining his programme. 'You're just making life difficult for me after everything I've done.' He wanted no negotiations. He just wanted the cheque written there and then.

Kevin was increasingly close to John Wardle. He knew the vice-chairman was the biggest investor in Manchester City and he would have been aware, too, that John was a man who was in awe of him and his achievements. John was very susceptible to Kevin's personality. This would present increasing problems for me. Ever since becoming chairman four years before, I had enjoyed the benefits of working with a completely united board. Now, as Kevin's demands for increased spending became ever more insistent, that unity would begin to fray. There began to be leaks to the press, just as there had been under Francis Lee. There would usually be only one theme to these headlines: Kevin Keegan needed more money. When City lost, Kevin would pinpoint a lack of funds as the reason behind the defeat.

Despite all the euphoria generated by the win over United in the Manchester derby, we lost the next match, 1-0 at home to Charlton. Keegan said in his post-match press conference: 'On today's evidence, Charlton look more likely to stay up than us. And that should be telling my board of directors that they need to make some decisions about our ambitions. Do the board have the same ambitions as me? You'd have to ask the chairman.'

City were not obviously in danger of relegation. After the Charlton defeat, we were 12th, five points clear of the drop zone. It was an odd subject for a manager, especially a manager so famed for his optimism, to raise. After beating Manchester United, he had talked about City qualifying for European football for the first time since 1978. A week later, we went to Middlesbrough, were beaten 3-1 and slipped to 15th. The headline in the *Manchester Evening News* was: 'Over to You, Mr Chairman'. Beneath the headline was the strapline: 'Keegan Needs Spending Money'. Above it was: 'City Need Reinforcements'.

In the September board meeting in which we had discussed our difficulties with the Co-op Bank, we had also discussed a planned securitisation loan that would be overseen by the American investment bank, Bear Stearns.

A securitisation loan was becoming a popular way to raise funds for football clubs. The loans were larger, longer- term and had lower rates of interest than could usually be offered by banks. They were guaranteed against the future revenue streams – usually season ticket sales – of the club. It was borrowing from tomorrow to pay for today.

The most famous securitisation loan had been taken out by Leeds United. At £60m, it was the largest loan ever made to an English football club. All the yearly revenue from season tickets and hospitality at Elland Road would be paid to the lenders on the first day of every September. It came to grief because it relied on Leeds playing in the Champions League and because the Leeds chairman, Peter Ridsdale, had authorised wild overspending on players to get them into European competition. It led directly to their financial disintegration and it was not coincidental that after 2003, when Leeds' finances were laid waste, no club took out a securitisation loan for three years. For a securitisation loan to work, costs had to be carefully monitored. The interest rates may have been comparatively low but it was not free money.

At £43m, Manchester City's securitisation loan would be considerably less than Leeds United's and would mainly be used for fitting out the City of Manchester Stadium and funding the club in the Premier League. The board minutes in September 2002 recorded that I stressed the club's wage bill should not exceed 60 per cent of its income. At Leeds in 2002, two-thirds of every pound the club raised was spent on its players. A year later, that had increased to 88 per cent, mainly because revenue streams at Elland Road were collapsing as Leeds fell out of European football.

The board minutes also recorded: 'The chairman confirmed that the understanding with the manager was that, unless we were doing extremely well, there would be no transfer funds in January 2003, although there would be some scope for investment in wages. For 2003/04 there would be £5m in cash (for wages) and £10m in transfer fees available. This would be communicated to the manager in the near future.'

Alistair Mackintosh was professional and reliable at producing cashflow models and financial reports but Keegan would come to board meetings and produce his own figures to demonstrate that we had done wonderfully well in the transfer market and thus had leeway to make further signings. These figures would invariably be wrong. Sometimes, they were absolute cobblers. Kevin stuck to his guns. Constructive dialogue became very difficult.

One day, Kevin came to me and Alistair with sheets of paper and scribbled notes, accompanied by Stuart Pearce, who I suppose was acting as his 'heavy'. He began laying out his papers in front of us and when we raised objections he pointed to me: 'Well I have to say, I don't trust you.' Then he pointed to Alistair and said: 'And I don't trust you.'

Chris Bird: We had lost 3-1 away to Middlesbrough and Kevin Keegan was sat there alone in the changing room. I asked if everything was all right and he said: 'No, that's it, I'm done.' I told him he wasn't resigning. He said he was and suggested I got hold of John Wardle and bring him down to the dressing rooms. When I refused, he asked me to tell the chairman. I suggested he got in his car, went home and saw what tomorrow brought. It would have been November 2002. A fortnight before, we had won the Manchester derby for the first time in 13 years.

Shaun Goater: My first thought when Nicolas Anelka was announced was that he would be brilliant to play alongside. I didn't see him as a threat, though

I knew I would have to work hard. It was what I wanted. I had come to Manchester City to play with global names. We had a great relationship. He knew everyone would be watching everything he did and that he would attract defenders and, if that gave me one defender to deal with, I'd be more than pleased. In the derby, we gave the fans something they had been longing for.

An Untenable Transfer

WHEN WRITING my Christmas message to Manchester City's supporters, I was in a buoyant mood. We were 12th in the Premier League and about to play Tottenham. As I reminded our fans, four years before City had been 12th in League Division Two, the lowest position in the club's history, having just lost to York.

'As Christmas 2002 approaches, the problems of 1998 seem a distant nightmare. We are months away from our move to the City of Manchester Stadium, for which we have already sold 31,000 season tickets. The club has professionals in every area and, of course, Kevin Keegan has taken our team to the middle of the Premier League. We have made considerable investments in our playing squad and have made funds available for the January transfer window. We should be in for an exciting 2003.'

Within three months of writing this, I had decided I could no longer continue as chairman of Manchester City. We had, despite the boardroom minutes in September, made some transfer funds available but not as much as Kevin wanted and the way he intended to use them to buy Robbie Fowler caused tensions within a previously united board, which I concluded had made my position untenable.

On paper, Manchester City did not seem a club in obvious need of a centre-forward. We had assembled six at the cost of £28.5m. Three of them, Nicolas Anelka, Jon Macken and Paulo Wanchope, had broken the club transfer record. Paulo, however, would miss the whole season with injury. Macken was seldom fit and would never be a prolific goalscorer for City – he would be sold to Crystal Palace in 2005 for a fifth of the fee we paid Preston. Darren Huckerby, like Wanchope, had been signed by Joe Royle. However, although Kevin had signed the teenaged Huckerby from Lincoln when he was at Newcastle, he made relatively little impact at St James' Park and it was the same at Maine Road. He scored one league goal for us that season – against Newcastle – and would be loaned out to Norwich the next. Matias Vuoso would not play a game.

That left Anelka and Shaun Goater. Even after scoring twice in the Manchester derby, Shaun always felt Keegan was looking for an excuse to drop him. Goater was left out for the Christmas fixtures in which Keegan played Anelka as a lone striker. Fulham were beaten at Craven Cottage, there was a draw with Everton and a 1-0 loss at home to Liverpool in the FA Cup. Goater was recalled for the league game with Leeds at Elland Road on 11 January and scored in a 2-1 victory. Shaun, however, felt Kevin's interest was more in another striker, who played just 28 minutes for Leeds and failed to score. Shaun and the rest of the City squad knew he wanted to sign Fowler.

Keegan was not a manager who developed his own players. At Newcastle, he had scrapped the reserve team. If he wanted a footballer, he would buy one. He wanted to buy Fowler. He had raised this in November. I had gone to Carrington to watch training and Kevin had come over and said: 'Do you want to sit down, chairman? I want to talk to you about something big.'

He wanted to talk about Robbie Fowler, the boy from Toxteth who at Liverpool had been one of the most natural goalscorers Anfield had ever seen. Against Arsenal in August 1994, at the age of 19, he had scored the Premier

League's swiftest hat-trick in four minutes and 33 seconds. Of all the strikers in Liverpool's history, only Ian Rush could boast a better goals-to-games ratio. Kevin thought he would make a perfect foil for Anelka.

Of course, I knew Fowler's reputation but when Kevin mentioned the fee, which was initially around £13m, I was immediately concerned. I wanted to take things slowly and slowly was not how Keegan worked. When we had this conversation in November 2002, Fowler had not played a match for Leeds in eight months. While the quality of Fowler's finishing may not have been in doubt, there had long been a sizeable question mark over his fitness.

Since suffering a serious knee injury in the Merseyside derby in March 1998, Fowler's career had fallen away. He was injured again when playing against Manchester United at Anfield 18 months later. He required an ankle operation that put him out for two months. On his return, he was found to require another operation because of calcification on the bone. He was out for four more months. In the summer of 2000, playing a pre-season game in Belfast, Fowler was injured in a collision with the Glentoran keeper. This cost him another month.

In addition to the frustration of injury upon injury, Fowler had no time for the Liverpool manager, Gérard Houllier. This was instrumental in his move to Leeds in November 2001. The fee was £12m, which Fowler thought excessive since he had only 18 months remaining on his contract. In March 2002, he suffered a hip injury which Fowler reflected did more damage to his career than any of the injuries he had sustained at Liverpool.

Leeds released his medical records fairly early on in the negotiations. When our medical staff studied his injury record, they came to me and said it was doubtful whether Fowler would ever again be the same player. Fowler did not return to the Leeds first team until 16 December 2002. He scored in a 3-0 win at Bolton but did not feel fully fit. Shortly afterwards, his manager, Terry Venables, informed Fowler that the club would be looking to sell him in the newly introduced January transfer window. Venables thought he and the England centre-half Jonathan Woodgate were the two players for whom Leeds could obtain a quick, sizeable fee.

We, however, were deeply split on the issue. Keegan, Makin and Wardle were keen on the deal. Because of Fowler's injury record and the need to fight unnecessary spending, I was not. I would find myself negotiating with

Peter Ridsdale, my manager and my own board, which made my position increasingly difficult. I told them that the medical evidence would not support the transfer, we should not pay an upfront fee and that, therefore, Fowler should be brought to City on a pay-per-play basis. Dennis Tueart was not helpful to me. He backed Keegan.

Daniel Taylor, writing in *The Guardian,* commented: 'It is understood David Bernstein's relations have become particularly strained with Dennis Tueart, regarded as Keegan's closest ally on the board and the man responsible for tempting him back into management. Keegan will not tolerate being in charge of a club that is not in a position to challenge for the title in the next three years.' Taylor pointed out that, in the summer of 2002, only one Premier League club – Manchester United – had spent more than City.

On 30 December, under the headline 'Wardle to Take Grip', the *Manchester Evening News* told its readers that the vice-chairman and Dennis would now be liaising with Keegan every day. The paper's sports editor, Peter Spencer, wrote: 'Keegan is not happy with mid-table consolidation and, like the majority of the fans, isn't bothered about balancing the books because he passionately believes an all-conquering team bringing back the glory days will make enough money to settle debt.' That sounded too much like what Leeds United had attempted to do, a policy that was now unravelling disastrously at Elland Road.

I would not block Kevin from signing the player but the fee – which was now £6.5m – needed to be restructured. The salary package we would be prepared to offer Fowler was around £780,000 a year less than he was being paid by Leeds. Ridsdale agreed to cover the difference by paying Fowler an additional £15,000 a week over the course of his contract with City.

I phoned Ridsdale, who was a man I knew and liked. I particularly remember his habit of serving different-coloured champagne in the boardroom at Elland Road in the days when he was 'living the dream'. Now, we spoke chairman to chairman and agreed a pay-per-play deal. It worked out at about one per cent of any proposed transfer fee. So, instead of paying Leeds £6.5m, we would have paid them £65,000 every time Fowler played.

That, to me, seemed a sensible decision. However, I was forced to compromise. If my board had remained solid and supported my negotiating position, I am sure we would have delivered this deal.

In the end, under pressure from my own board, we agreed to a fee of £3m and another £3m based on appearances.

When I was negotiating transfers, Kevin liked to say to me: 'Chairman, the problem is I like going through the front door and you like going through the back door.' By that, he meant I should slap the asking fee on the table without bothering to investigate any alternatives, which to him would be too slow and cumbersome.

This was a prime example. Keegan strongly objected to my having gone behind his back to intervene in the transfer, despite the fact it had led to a far better deal for Manchester City. He thought it undermined him. When I insisted Fowler should have an absolutely thorough medical, Kevin accused me of 'treating this footballer like a piece of meat'. The fact was that Leeds were desperate to get Fowler and his salary off their books. When Fowler made his comeback at Bolton, Leeds were 16th in the Premier League, two points off a relegation place. They had no chance of reaching the Champions League, which would have given them some kind of lifeline. Leeds had no choice but to take any kind of deal for Robbie.

What complicated matters was that we were also negotiating with Bordeaux for their 28-year-old centre-half,

David Sommeil. The fee would be £3m. On 14 January, I convened a board meeting at Maine Road to raise my concerns at how financially exposed Manchester City would be if the two transfers went through. The board minutes recorded: 'A revised cashflow forecast was tabled with updated assumptions. That showed that, if Fowler and Sommeil were purchased, it would contribute to a level of borrowings between November 2003 and March 2004 in excess of our facilities ... the effect of the two transactions would be to commit club funds to the extent of £9m over the next two years.'

In November, the board had agreed that our borrowings should be limited to £5m. John Wardle then pledged that he and David Makin would lend the club an additional £4m. I told him that it was probable that all of that money would be required over the next 12 months.

Fowler underwent what he described as the most thorough medical of his life, supervised by our physio, Rob Harris. It lasted 12 hours. Afterwards, the deal appeared to have collapsed. Fowler announced he would be staying with Leeds. The headline in the *Manchester Evening News* on 17 January was 'What A Mess'. Their Manchester City correspondent, Chris Bailey, told his readers that Wardle had been shuttling between my office and Kevin's and was now taking up a more 'hands-on' role at the club. Kevin knew Wardle was the key shareholder and was putting pressure on him that John was unable to resist.

The *Evening News* published a feature over two pages headlined 'Who's in Charge?' Bailey wrote: 'This week's events should tell supporters that there is room for only one sheriff at Manchester City and the powers that be should decide very quickly who they want wearing the badge. Chairman David Bernstein and manager Kevin Keegan have quite clearly ended their honeymoon period and one of them might just be about to climb on his horse and ride out of town.' Another newspaper described Keegan as 'blazing mad'. He was said to blame my intervention for the failure of the deal.

The decision to pull out of the transfer had been Fowler's. Chris Bailey may have written that Keegan 'had set his heart and soccer soul on landing Fowler' but Kevin had yet to have a proper conversation with Robbie. Fowler found this strange and felt that, with three years left on his contract, he may have been leaving Leeds too quickly. Much more importantly and despite all their previous differences, Gérard Houllier, whose tactic of replacing Anelka with El-Hadji Diouf had gone badly wrong, phoned Fowler to ask if he wanted to go back to Liverpool. This excited Fowler enough to tell Houllier that he would be willing to take a wage cut to return to Anfield – something he was not prepared to do to play at Maine Road.

However, Houllier discovered through his chief executive, Rick Parry, that the Liverpool board would not pay the Leeds asking price of £5m and thought the player too much of a risk. Fowler recalls a Leeds director going over to him at the training ground at Thorp Arch and telling him to 'take the money and run, son, because this club is going under'. It seemed like good advice. He arranged a meeting with Keegan and was enthused by the way Manchester City was sold to him. Leeds sold him on the terms I had agreed. Fowler quickly discovered Leeds' promise to pay him an additional £15,000 a week was not forthcoming.

Fowler made his debut for Manchester City on 1 February against West Bromwich Albion. The chairman's seat in the directors' box at Maine Road was next to a low wall, the other side of which sat season ticket holders, whose faces I knew well. As City came out, their attack led by Anelka and Fowler, one of them said to me: 'Chairman, you must be so proud to see this when you think of where we were when you took over.' I replied: 'We'll see after the match how proud I feel.'

West Brom won 2-1. Neither Anelka nor Fowler scored. Our goal was an own goal. When summing up his first two seasons at Manchester City, Fowler recalled: 'I played like a cabbage.'

In September 2004, Paul Hince, the chief sportswriter of the *Manchester Evening News*, summed up his feelings about a footballer who, he wrote, had been 'put on planet Earth to score goals'. By then, Fowler's tally for Manchester City had been 15 goals in 50 appearances. 'The Fowler in his pomp at Anfield wouldn't have been happy with twice that amount,' Hince wrote. 'It was his reading of the situations in and around the opponents' penalty area and that little burst of pace that took him into a goal-scoring position.

'The Fowler of today will still see those situations developing ahead of his opponents but, as a result of those serious injuries, his legs no longer obey his brain. That is the essential spark in his game which has been extinguished. My guess – and I hope I'm wrong – is that, at the age of 29, that spark of genius is gone forever.' It was cold comfort to read the conclusion of the piece: 'What the past 20 months have shown is that Bernstein was right all along.'

At the same time as the Fowler transfer was progressing, I felt that now Manchester City were back in the Premier League, the management structure of the club needed sharpening up. My two key people had been Chris Bird and Alistair Mackintosh. Alistair had shown himself to be a shrewd, able performer. He was excellent at representing the club in a professional way when we were dealing with the council or the bankers. I thought he should be promoted to chief executive. Chris had a different set of skills and I thought he could have a role in the international development of Manchester City, while continuing with his role as head of communications and being a key member of the team. The two were very close; Chris had been best man at Alistair's wedding.

Once I had made this decision, I met with John Wardle to get his approval. John was very positive. However, when Chris objected to Alistair being promoted above him, David Makin, who was very friendly with Chris, supported him. This led to John changing his position. Chris then resigned, which left me in a difficult situation. Making Alistair chief executive had been my decision. Now, I had lost Bird and Makin was unhappy. In the background, Keegan was expressing his unhappiness that City could not match his spending requirements. The Wardle–Makin loan of £6.15m was due to be paid off in 12 monthly instalments, starting on 30 June 2003. There would be even less money for Keegan to spend and his dissatisfaction was only likely to grow.

Suddenly, things started to fragment. The divisions at the top of the club were now being leaked to the press. My position as chairman had always been potentially precarious because I was not a significant shareholder in the club and I was not providing the finance. I also cared too much about Manchester City to risk a repeat of the divisions that had so undermined Peter Swales and Francis Lee. There was now a threat that Wardle and Makin might cease to be supportive. I had to ask John to write a letter of support to me, which would have been unthinkable 12 months before. He did but the writing was on the wall.

I am aware that some people might have been tempted to hang on as chairman of Manchester City. However, I was commuting between London and Manchester, making certain sacrifices in terms of seeing my family, but loving the job. Suddenly, I had thoughts that travelling up to Manchester was not a journey I wanted to make. I used to relish the train journey from Euston to Piccadilly. Now,

I was fighting against my own manager and my own main shareholders; leaks were getting into the press and it would only get worse. I did not mind tough negotiations; in my business life I had dealt with many difficult and powerful people. However, I did like to think that my back was covered and at Manchester City I no longer had that impression.

It was the antithesis of everything our teamwork had built in the previous five years. It was like we had climbed a mountain and now I felt the supports were being removed and there was a deep and dangerous drop below. I would have loved to have taken Manchester City into their new home and perhaps to have carried on until we found a major investor, like the people from Abu Dhabi.

However, in life you can rarely choose a Hollywood ending. If I wanted to stay ahead of the game, I needed to get out, but it was not an easy decision to make. In March 2003, I decided to resign. In my resignation statement, delivered on 5 March, I pointed out that the decision to leave Manchester City was entirely my own.

It went on: 'On my appointment in 1998, I emphasised three factors required to fulfil the chairman's role effectively – unity, stability and professionalism. Until recently, my board, major shareholders and key employees have successfully worked together to achieve these. Over the last few months, there has been a divergence of views on fundamental strategic issues, particularly concerning finance and management structures. I believe this has inhibited my ability to direct the club in the way I would wish.

'During my five years as chairman, the club has made outstanding progress. We have advanced from the depths of the Third Division to mid-table in the Premier League. We are only months away from moving into our new stadium and have developed an outstanding training ground. We have an excellent squad of players, in which we have made a considerable investment, and an outstanding team of people employed at the club. Manchester City is respected and stands on the brink of real achievement.

'I would like to thank our wonderful fans for their backing. They have been fantastic in their support, which has never wavered even during the most difficult times. I have been touched by their kindness and enthusiasm. I have supported Manchester City since I was a boy and I am desperate for us to succeed. I wish the club well and hope that it will build on the solid foundations that have been laid.'

Chris Bird: I always imagined this would be a five-year job, that I would probably have a season at the City of Manchester Stadium and then go back to working for myself. I thought David had gone behind my back to make Alistair Mackintosh chief executive. My secretary – who was also Alistair's secretary – knew there was something going on because she was aware of meetings I wasn't being invited to. I didn't think I could work with David, a man who I would have walked over hot coals for, because my trust in him had gone.

Dennis Tueart: When David left, the solidarity in the boardroom collapsed. David had been part of the boardroom group who in the five years from 1998 had dragged the club from what would have been a slow death into building the solid foundations of what it is now.

Dave Wallace: David was prudent, he steadied the ship and he gave us our Manchester City back. It started the rise to what we are now and I dread to think where we would be without him.

Shaun Goater: I didn't want to leave City. In pre-season (the summer of 2003), I was being told that Reading really wanted me and that the club had agreed a deal, but I wanted to stay and fight for my spot. Then I was told that I wouldn't play. In pre-season, we went to Denmark and played teams like Ajax but I didn't play a minute – and that was to force me to leave. I didn't want that. I loved the club and everything about it. I wasn't afraid of the challenge, whether I was fighting for a place with Nicolas Anelka or Robbie Fowler. I welcomed those kinds of challenges. I had no choice about leaving.

Epilogue: Into the Arms of a Dictator

IN FOOTBALL, departing chairmen are seldom thanked. Many of them might consider they were lucky to escape in one piece. My two predecessors at Manchester City had, more or less, been driven out.

I received neither hate nor jeers when I went but I was sent armfuls of letters, emails and cards from people in Manchester and beyond, from people I knew and those I had never met, telling me they regretted my decision while recognising what I had done for the club. I kept every one of them. Of all the things I had done in my career, this had been the best.

'Please don't feel a failure,' wrote one woman from Fallowfield. There was a letter from the rector of the Holy Trinity Church on Platt Lane and another from Colin Shindler, who wrote: 'I am attaching just one of a dozen letters I've had with similar sentiments. There is a huge groundswell of popular feeling on your side – the best evidence you could possibly wish for as evidence of the success of your tenure. If you want to storm the barricades, I think you'd win but, being the honourable mensch you are, I doubt that would be your preferred option. It has been wonderful to know that the club has been in such unselfish hands. I shudder to think what lies ahead.'

Colin was not the only one to be concerned about the future. From his home in the Wirral, the Everton chairman, Philip Carter, wrote to me: 'I appreciate only too well your philosophy regarding the financial control necessary to maintain long-term stability and your decision not to compromise your standpoint. Too many clubs have and will be entering the murky waters of administration over the next few years and sound advice will be at a premium.'

Football was enduring a hugely unstable time. Between April 2001 and June 2003, eight clubs that had been members of the Premier League would fall into administration. They included Wimbledon, who had once offered us their place in the top flight in return for a merger and who had found a new home not in Dublin or Manchester but Milton Keynes. Ipswich Town, who had so joyfully celebrated their return to European football on the night we were relegated, were also among those who had fallen apart financially. Leeds, against all the odds, held out until 2007, by which time they had been relegated to the third tier of English football.

Relegation from the Premier League was too often a financial death sentence and, of the teams in the top division in March 2003, only seven would avoid the drop over the next two decades. We would be among that group, along with Manchester United, Liverpool, Arsenal, Chelsea, Tottenham and Everton.

I did not go back to Maine Road to see Manchester City bid farewell to their old home. My last game there had been a 5-1 defeat to Arsenal that had seen Arsène Wenger's side four up inside 20 minutes and Richard Dunne ask his manager if he could be substituted before half-time. The result and the style of Arsenal's victory carried echoes of 2001 but, two years on, Manchester City were a much better team and were never seriously in danger of relegation. Our time at Maine Road fizzled out with 1-0 defeats to West Ham and Southampton but earlier victories at Tottenham and Liverpool ensured City ended their final season at Maine Road in ninth place. It was two positions better than in their first season at Maine Road in 1923/24 and their best finish since 1993, when I was first approached to take an active interest in Manchester City and the slogans proclaimed 'Forward with Franny'.

It was painful not to be officially involved when the City of Manchester Stadium opened its doors to us but I did go to City's first league game there on 23 August. I did so anonymously, walked to the stadium and took my seat in the stands. We watched a last-minute goal from David Sommeil rescue a point against Portsmouth. The people sitting around me were supportive.

So were some more unlikely people. I was attending a lunch at a London hotel off the Edgware Road, where George Best and Sir Bobby Charlton were on the top table. Bobby saw me and came through the room. 'David, I am very sorry to see that you have left Manchester City,' he said. 'But, in another way, I am really rather pleased, as you were getting the club's act together so well. We were getting worried.'

Bobby would have been rather less pleased when watching City win the Manchester derby 4-1 at Eastlands in March. Kevin Keegan oversaw some spectacular victories at our new home, with Bolton beaten 6-2 and Everton 5-1 on the final afternoon of the season, although that last day had begun with Manchester City in 17th place. Results had been horribly erratic.

None was more erratic and more 'typically City' than the FA Cup fourth-round replay at Tottenham on 4 February 2004. I had gone to White Hart Lane with my boys as a fan, sitting behind one of the goals with the City supporters and at half-time our team was three goals behind and down to ten men after Joey Barton had been sent off for arguing with the referee as the players walked off for the interval. Nicolas Anelka had already been forced off with injury. In the away dressing room, Keegan told his assistant, Derek Fazackerley, that, if the tie continued like this, he expected to be dismissed. City had not won a league game in three months.

And yet a depleted team fought back to score an improbable four in the second half. Jon Macken, who had replaced Anelka, put away a last-minute winner in front of two sets of fans, neither of whom could quite believe what they had seen. It was a thrilling, magical spectacle and yet, afterwards, I did reflect that, if Tottenham had ended the tie six goals to the good and Keegan had gone, I might have come back to Manchester City. They were fleeting thoughts. In August 2005, I was sent a letter from John Wardle, who had replaced me as chairman, saying my passes for the directors' box would not be renewed. That

I was denied a pass to a stadium I helped to create upset me greatly.

Wardle, who had been persuaded to take over by Keegan, was not an obvious front man and it did not seem he was enjoying his tenure. His first annual general meeting was not a comfortable one. He insisted to his shareholders that the club was not going the way of Leeds United while admitting there was now little money for Keegan to spend.

This might have come as a surprise to Kevin. He had known Wardle was the money man at Manchester City and he knew, too, that John was a fan of his. However, if he thought Wardle might continue to fund him in the same way Sir John Hall had done at Newcastle, he was to be disappointed.

Wardle and David Makin's sports goods business, JD Sports, was by now coming under real pressure. It was being squeezed at the top end of its market by JJB Sports, owned by the Wigan chairman Dave Whelan and at the bottom end by the aggressive sales tactics of Mike Ashley's Sports Direct. In May 2005, Wardle and Makin sold their shares in JD Sports to Stephen Rubin at Pentland for £45m. That might seem a lot of money but it was something of a knockdown price. Nearly 20 years later, JD Sports would be valued in the billions. Neither John nor David was good in a crisis and would not have relished fighting simultaneously on the football and the business front.

The money Wardle had been able to give Keegan had not been used well. Dennis Tueart, who had initially supported the Robbie Fowler transfer, thought the decision to add Steve McManaman to the mix absurd, given the player was 30 and barely playing for Real Madrid, where he was being paid £60,000 a week. Dennis was proved right by a series of desultory performances.

As well as Fowler and McManaman, Keegan went for experienced players with little resale value such as David Seaman and David James to replace Peter Schmeichel. Anelka, who even by his standards was becoming increasingly disaffected, was sold to Fenerbahce in January 2005 for £7m. Three months later, increasingly unable to motivate himself, Keegan decided to quit.

His departure had echoes of his leaving of Newcastle eight years before. He felt unable to work with the financial restrictions placed upon him and asked Wardle if he could resign at the end of the season. Wardle, like Newcastle's Freddie Fletcher in 1997, told him he was not in favour of long goodbyes. Stuart Pearce took over and steered City to an eighth-place finish. Had Fowler not missed a penalty in the final match against Middlesbrough, they would have qualified for the UEFA Cup.

That was as good as it got. City finished 15th the following season and 14th in 2007 after failing to score a league goal at home between 13 January and 5 May. When Pearce was dismissed, the press was briefed that Manchester City's football had become intolerably boring. By then, however, the structure of the club was about to change irrevocably.

As Manchester City began running out of money, potential investors began gathering like bees around a honeypot. Francis Lee was said to be putting together a consortium to return to the club. Ray Ranson, who had been Manchester City's right-back in the 1981 FA Cup final and had subsequently made a fortune in the insurance business, made a bid for the club, valuing Manchester City at £90m. He would offer Wardle £20m to repay the loans he had made to the club and provide £20m for players. His bid was rejected by John, who did decide to sell out to a man with absolutely no connection to Manchester City and who was said to have blood on his hands.

Thaksin Shinawatra was the son of a politician and businessman from Chiang Mai in northern Thailand. He was educated in Texas and became a lieutenant colonel in the Thai police before making millions in the telecoms industry. In February 2001, at the head of a party he had founded, he became prime minister of Thailand. Once elected, Shinawatra fought against rural poverty, promoted universal healthcare and pushed a public building programme that included the reconstruction of Bangkok's main airport.

However, his opponents accused him of endemic corruption and of unlawfully killing thousands in his 'War on Drugs'. In September 2006, while he was at a conference in New York, Shinawatra was deposed by a military coup and went into exile in London. He was believed to have assets of £800m and had already made attempts to buy Fulham and Liverpool. He would shortly be joined by his wife, who had been convicted of tax evasion.

Three months after being forced from office, Shinawatra bid for Manchester City, valuing the club at £81.6m, of which nearly three-quarters was debt. By June 2007, he had acquired three-quarters of the club, paying Wardle and Makin £21.6m for their 29.9 per cent stake and repaying £17.5m of their loans to Manchester City. The big losers were

City's small shareholders because they were forced to sell at 40p a share, which was an undervaluation. The following month, once Shinawatra had bought up 90 per cent of the club, his offer became unconditional, which meant you had to sell to him. There were no other circumstances in which I would have done so.

I did not see how Shinawatra could have passed the Premier League's 'fit and proper persons test' to become owner of a club. I did consider leading a bid to block his takeover by buying Sky Sports' 9.9 per cent stake which, together with my shares, would have prevented Shinawatra passing the 90 per cent threshold that would enable him to buy every share in the club. However, I concluded that I would be seen as a disgruntled ex-chairman attempting to halt what would be seen in some quarters as progress.

At first, things seemed to be going very well. Wardle and Alistair Mackintosh were asked to remain on the board. Sven-Göran Eriksson, who had been in charge of England 12 months before, agreed to become manager. With a month to go before the start of the season, Sven brought in a flurry of foreign players whom he admitted he had seen only on video. Some, like the Brazilians Elano and Geovanni, produced some thrilling moments. Graduates of Jim Cassell's academy, such as Michael Johnson and Micah Richards, came to the fore. Joe Hart became Manchester City's most convincing goalkeeper since Joe Corrigan. For the first time since 1970, Manchester United were beaten home and away. Free Thai food was handed out in Albert Square. City fans called their new owner 'Frank' as, to Mancunian ears, Shinawatra sounded a bit like 'Sinatra'. As Eriksson discovered when invited to a karaoke club by his boss, Shinawatra rather fancied himself as a singer.

It could not last. Sven soon discovered that Shinawatra also fancied himself as a football guru and would phone him to give advice on how to motivate his team. Then Thaksin's assets were frozen by corruption investigations in Thailand. Wardle was asked for three loans of £2m, money he was never to get back. Manchester City tumbled down the table. Eriksson was told he would be dismissed at the end of the season. The players initially refused to start the final match, at Middlesbrough. When they did, City were thrashed, 8-1.

By August 2008, Manchester City were headed for the financial rocks until, out of the blue, they were taken over by a consortium from the United Arab Emirates called Abu Dhabi United, backed by its government. They were suddenly the richest club in the world. Perhaps the only advantage of Shinawatra's takeover is that when Abu Dhabi launched their bid, they only had to deal with one man. Had they had to negotiate with the old club structure, with its fragmented shareholdings, their bid would have taken far longer to succeed, though I believe it was too good ever to have been rejected. However, the profit on that deal went to Shinawatra when it should have gone to Manchester City's small shareholders, who had been forced to sell at 40p a share.

The defining point of the Abu Dhabi era was the 94th-minute winner from Sergio Aguero against Queens Park Rangers that won Manchester City the title on the final afternoon of the 2011/12 season. From Paul Dickov's ridiculously late goal in the play-off final at Wembley to Aguero's stoppage-time intervention at what was now the Etihad Stadium was 13 years. It had been a winding road.

To some, like Colin Shindler, the arrival of the Arab money meant the end of their time supporting Manchester City. Colin felt it no longer had any connection to the city in which it was located. It was another club entirely. Colin found himself in a minority. To me and to many others, it was a continuation of the club that had enthralled me so many years ago. You cannot run football on nostalgia.

City had taken an explosive step up in an age when Premier League clubs became increasingly foreign-owned, although no other foreign owner copied what the government of Abu Dhabi did by funding the regeneration of the community around their stadium as happened in east Manchester. Under Pep Guardiola, the football eclipsed even the golden age of Joe Mercer and Malcolm Allison.

One thing that did seem to go was the saying 'Typical City'. To anybody under 30, the phrase carries no resonance. Nobody of that age would have an inkling of just how regularly Manchester City once snatched defeat from the jaws of victory. They would see 'Typical City' as being a byword for winning trophies with style and a certain inevitability.

Before the takeovers, first by Shinawatra and then by Abu Dhabi, there were people asking me to return to Manchester City, but the only time I went back into club football was when I joined the board at Aston Villa. I had, by then, stepped down as chairman of the FA and, in March 2016, I was asked if I would join the board by the Aston Villa owner, Randy Lerner. The club was in a desperate state, bottom of the Premier League and a dozen points from safety. Relegation was almost inevitable. Joining me on the board were Mervyn King, the former chairman of the Bank of England who was an Aston Villa fan, and the club's former manager, Brian Little.

Our task was to have been restructuring the club after relegation in much the same way as I had done at Manchester City. Given that Aston Villa had a far superior stadium and training ground than City possessed in 1998 and were heading into the second rather than the third tier, it ought to have been a more obviously straightforward task. However, Lerner showed absolutely no interest in engaging with us. The relationship lasted a month or two before Mervyn and I jointly resigned and was best summed up by a trans-Atlantic phone call in which Lerner told me: 'David, you may think you know something about football but I once employed five managers in one year.' My response that I had employed two managers in five years did not go down too well.

Club football had changed in the 13 years since I had been chairman of Manchester City. Contracts had grown ever more lucrative and complex; the scale of the Premier League club was forever expanding. In my time at City, you could make a difference with a clever deal here or shaving £500,000 off a project there. You could no longer, as I had done at Maine Road, ask a company to repair your stadium roof in return for a hospitality package. Clubs then were on a manageable scale. They did not aspire to become international conglomerates.

David Davies, the FA's former chief executive, invited me to a dinner at the headquarters of Coutts Bank in the Strand. He had also invited Sir Geoff Hurst. The room was full of high-powered people and the conversation was all about deals, franchising and monetising. I had to interrupt the conversation to remind people that we had with us the man whose goals had won England the World Cup and nobody had asked him a word about football.

> **Alistair Mackintosh:** John Wardle and David Makin were putting in money and, as chief executive, I was very protective of their money. I got the feeling that John and David began feeling quite well off and ended the process feeling quite poor, both because of how much they had invested in the club and how much the Premier League was developing at the time. Loans of several million pounds were once substantial sums of money and now they were small packages with so much money spinning around in the game. John and David could see that, which is why they decided to sell their shares to Thaksin.

I left Manchester City just before the Abu Dhabi takeover. Thaksin was quite a hands-on chairman; he was interested in the commercial and the football side of the business. There was a sense of excitement about the signings and about having Sven as manager. The only thing that could have wrecked City financially would be relegation and we were never seriously in danger of that. I remember standing outside Macclesfield's ground, where we were playing a pre-season friendly, and negotiating the sale of Shaun Wright-Phillips to Chelsea. We had held out against Arsenal, who were offering a fraction of the £21m Chelsea eventually paid and, under Roman Abramovich, Chelsea paid their transfer fees in one go.

When I go back to the Etihad Stadium with Fulham [where Alistair has been chief executive since 2008], there are so many warm memories. Looking at Manchester City now is a tribute to David. When he became chairman, with the club in perhaps the worst state in its history, he said Manchester should be like Milan and have two huge clubs competing for the city's attention. It has happened and I have been fortunate enough to have been part of that journey.

Dennis Tueart: Once Alistair Mackintosh became chief executive, I should have left. Alistair was brilliant with inanimate objects, like balance sheets. It was why he was so good negotiating for the new stadium but he was not a people person. When we were negotiating contracts, Alistair would often ask me to join him to meet with the agents. I suppose it was because he didn't do small talk well. What he would do would be to go through the fine detail of the contracts.

I was eventually sent an email with my resignation letter attached. There was no word of thanks or acknowledgement for the ten years I had put into the club. I was, however, extremely proud of what David and the board of directors had achieved in those five years which allowed the club to develop into what it is now.

Chris Bird: There is still a sense of 'Typical City' at the club managed by Pep Guardiola, the one that has dominated English football. Way back then, the phrase didn't mean we'd lose every week, it meant City would disappoint when we'd least expect it. There are still 'Typical City' moments, they are just a lot rarer. The DNA of the club hasn't changed. Losing to Tottenham in the Champions League quarter-final was 'Typical City', losing the Champions League Final to Chelsea was 'Typical City'. The supporters haven't changed; they just go to bigger games.

Dave Wallace: I don't think any Premier League club is what it was 20 years ago. Manchester City needed to be a new club, it had to change and the move to what is now the Etihad was instrumental. Now, you get fans from the Far East taking selfies and those wearing half-and-half scarves, though I think that's a good addition to the club. There's a bit of youth and a bit of sparkle there. It's a different club and it's a miles better club.

'Typical City' hasn't disappeared. 'Typical City' was winning the league in 1937 and being relegated the following year. Some of that is still here. Losing the FA Cup Final to an already-relegated Wigan in 2013 was 'Typical City'. You could also say it was 'Typical City' when we won the league with Aguero's last kick of the season in 2012 after going 2-1 down to a QPR side that had absolutely nothing to play for and who were down to ten men when Joey Barton got himself sent off. All clubs have 'Typical City' moments but we tend to be more self-deprecating. In the year we won the Treble, we were still singing: 'We never win at home and we never win away.'

Shaun Goater: The trajectory of the club since I left was amazing. When I left in 2003, Anelka would have been the one world-class player. Robbie had been a great striker but it took him the best part of a season and a half to get himself fit. Now at City there are world-class players everywhere you look. We were a family club because you knew all the staff and now we are a global club. We have gone from being a corner shop to Harrods. People still call out 'Feed the Goat' to me and it puts a smile on my face. It has been so many years since I played for City and it's lovely I am still appreciated.

When I came to Maine Road, all I wanted was that, when I left, people would say: 'He was a good player and he did his best for us.'

Dennis Tueart: When the final whistle blew in the Champions League Final in Istanbul and we had won the European Cup, I was very emotional. When I started watching Manchester City in about 1968, they were champions of England and one of the most glamorous clubs in Europe. When I joined City in 1974, it was still a significant force but, in all the years since then, Manchester City had been through so much and now, here we were. We had come full circle.

Afterword

VILLA PARK provided me with one of my fondest football memories. In the summer of 2012, I was chairman of the FA and, because Wembley was being used for the Olympic football tournament, the Community Shield between Chelsea and Manchester City had been switched to Villa Park. For the first time since 1968, Manchester City were champions and, as I walked on to the pitch to be introduced to the two teams, the City fans began chanting: 'There's only one David Bernstein.' For a moment, there was a tear in my eye.

Football may not be unique but it is at the sharpest end of sport. It is the world game operating on a huge stage. The wonder, well illustrated by the pyramid of English football, is the passion at every level. Huge crowds at Premier League matches show the same devotion to their club as 500 fans attending a match in the National League North. Being involved was a privilege; becoming chairman of Manchester City was a lifetime high but also represented a potential quicksand. One needs to share this passion but keep a cool and dispassionate head. It is important to be able to form close relationships with managers and players but put aside emotion when tough decisions have to be made. To enjoy success but to be able to deal with the inevitable periods of failure. To face your public, the fans, every matchday 50 times a year knowing that two or three bad results can instigate a crisis. Who would want to face all these challenges knowing the laurels for success are focused on the pitch but the finger of failure often points to the board? I certainly did and I would not have missed the experience for anything. We were really there.

Bibliography

Edghill, Richard: *Once A Blue, Always A Blue* (Pitch Publishing, 2014)

Eriksson, Sven-Göran: *My Story* (Headline, 2013)

Fowler, Robbie: *My Autobiography* (Pan Macmillan, 2007)

Goater, Shaun: *Feed the Goat* (The History Press, 2006)

Horton, Brian: *Two Thousand Games: A Life in Football* (Pitch Publishing, 2020)

Houllier, Gérard: *Je Ne Marcherai Jamais Seul* (Hugo Sport, 2015)

Keegan, Kevin: *My Life in Football* (Macmillan, 2018)

Rich, Tim: *Caught Beneath the Landslide* (deCoubertin Books, 2018)

Royle, Joe: *The Autobiography* (BBC Books, 2005)

Schmeichel, Peter: *One* (Hodder & Stoughton, 2021)

Tueart, Dennis: *My Football Journey* (Vision Sports Publishing, 2011)

Newspapers and magazines: *Manchester Evening News*, *The Independent*, *The Guardian*, *Daily Mirror*, *Daily Express*, *Mail on Sunday*, *The King of the Kippax*.